I0824371

The Gravel Garden

The Gravel Garden

Visionary, Drought-Defying, Naturalistic Designs

Jeff Epping *and* Teresa Woodard

Photography by Bob Stefko

TIMBER PRESS
Portland, Oregon

Photo credits appear on page 308.

Timber Press
Workman Publishing
Hachette Book Group, Inc.
1290 Avenue of the Americas
New York, New York 10104
timberpress.com

Timber Press is an imprint of Workman Publishing, a division of Hachette Book Group, Inc. The Timber Press name and logo are registered trademarks of Hachette Book Group, Inc.

Printed in Shenzhen, China (APO), on responsibly sourced paper
Text and cover design by Sarah Crumb and Hillary Caudle

ISBN 978-1-64326-482-0
A catalog record for this book is available from the Library of Congress.

CONTENTS

INTRODUCTION 7

Gravel at Home

Gravel Garden Blueprint 12
Jeff Epping; Madison, Wisconsin

Prairie-Inspired Garden with a Sense of Place . . 30
Ana and Ed McCracken; Ames, Iowa

Spouse's Loving Tribute 46
Mike Cunningham; Madison, Wisconsin

Plantsman's New Palette 62
Andrew Bunting; Swarthmore, Pennsylvania

Renovated Retreat 76
Sean Conway; Tiverton, Rhode Island

Gravel in the City

New Spin for a Roundabout 92
Swarthmore College; Swarthmore, Pennsylvania

The Power of Public Beautification 108
City of Madison; Madison, Wisconsin

New Potential for Vacant Lots 122
City of Chicago; Chicago, Illinois

Early Lessons from Dry Landscapes 136
Cassian Schmidt; Weinheim, Germany

Gravel in American Public Gardens

Technique Trailblazer 152
Olbrich Botanical Gardens; Madison, Wisconsin

Resilient Beauty 166
Meadowbrook Farm; Jenkintown, Pennsylvania

Creative Masterpiece 180
Chanticleer Garden; Wayne, Pennsylvania

Terraced Showcase 196
Reiman Gardens; Ames, Iowa

Living Laboratory in the Deep South 210
Stephen F. Austin State University; Nacogdoches, Texas

Gravel in British Public Gardens

Car Park to Paradise 226
Beth Chatto Gardens; Essex, England

Beacon of Creativity and Hope 236
Prospect Cottage; Dungeness, England

Delos Revival 248
Sissinghurst Castle Garden; Kent, England

Rewilded Walled Garden 260
Knepp Castle; West Sussex, England

Gravel at Work

Massive Rooftop Solution 276
Epic Headquarters; Verona, Wisconsin

Sustainable Statement 290
Argonne National Laboratory; Lemont, Illinois

ACKNOWLEDGMENTS 306

PHOTO CREDITS 308

RESOURCES 309

INDEX 311

Why Gravel Gardens? Why Now?

I'm often asked the question, "Gravel gardens? They sound so harsh, dry, and colorless and I love my green grass, so why would I want to replace it with a gravel garden?" While the name might not do it justice, the gardens are as beautiful as any garden out there. You'll be amazed by how easy they are to maintain and how many butterflies and birds they attract. Gravel gardens are great on so many levels.

Basically, gravel gardening is a technique in which deep-rooted, drought-tolerant perennials are planted in about a 6-inch layer of gravel that suppresses weeds and conserves water. In this book, we explore the art of gravel gardening, a naturalistic approach that holds so much promise for the future of ecological landscaping. We'll look at various scales and applications of gravel gardens, from intimate home settings to expansive public and commercial spaces. Through the examination of twenty remarkable gravel gardens, each distinguished by beauty and purpose, we hope to inspire and guide you to create your own beautiful garden with the resilience necessary to stand up to our changing climate. As gardeners, we possess the skills and opportunities to make a difference—one garden at a time.

Discovering Gravel Gardens

The concept of gravel gardening isn't new, although it is not as widely discussed as it ought to be. I was lucky enough to learn of it nearly thirty years ago when I visited Beth Chatto's iconic garden in England. I'll never forget her passion as she guided our group through her gravel garden, explaining why she created it and how it evolved over the years. She told us that this part of England was much drier than most others, and she didn't feel right using precious groundwater to irrigate the garden to keep it looking good. With that in mind, she designed a revolutionary new garden, using drought-tolerant plant species that would thrive with only natural rainfall, yet be as beautiful as any thirstier species. I was a relatively inexperienced gardener then, and was most captivated by how beautiful the garden was—I'm not sure I fully appreciated the impact of her environmentally conscious approach.

About ten years after seeing the Chatto garden, I found myself once again inspired—this time here in Wisconsin, by my friend and colleague Roy Diblik. Roy, a well-renowned plantsman and garden designer, had just returned from Germany where he toured the botanical gardens of Hermannshof with our friend, the noted garden designer Piet Oudolf, and Hermannshof's innovative designer, Cassian Schmidt. Cassian's North American Prairie Garden fascinated Roy the most—not the plants themselves, which he knew well, but the medium they were planted in: gravel. Cassian's gravel garden sparked Roy's curiosity, and he returned home inspired, eager to try a similar approach. A month or two later, I stopped to see Roy and he took me straight to his new gravel garden. I admit, it didn't look all that exciting; honestly, it looked more like a parking lot than a garden. But his enthusiasm was contagious, and soon I was asking him about how to build one. Upon leaving, I told him that I was going to try one somewhere soon, but quite honestly, I thought I'd wait a year or two to see how his garden turned out.

Designing My First Gravel Gardens

The opportunity finally came a couple of years later when I designed a gravel garden for Epic Systems in 2008, then another at Olbrich Botanical Gardens a year later, where I was director of horticulture. Though I was new to the concept and made plenty of mistakes, these gardens exceeded my expectations tenfold. Never had I gardened so easily and experienced such amazing results! Not only were they as beautiful as any garden I'd ever designed, but they were also incredibly easy to care for. After a few years, the gravel gardens needed no irrigation, fertilizer, or mulch, and weeds were virtually nonexistent. Read that sentence again: no irrigation! No fertilizer! No mulch! While they required more work to construct at the outset, the payoff was well worth the extra effort. Each spring, all they needed was a simple cleanup. I now understood Beth's vision, not just for creating beauty but for caring for the earth at the same time. Like her, Cassian, and Roy, I was excited to share this technique with others.

I began writing articles, teaching classes, and giving lectures on gravel gardening, and each time I was delighted by the excitement it sparked in others. Many people I met wanted to reduce their "lawnprints" and replace them with more eco-friendly gardens but worried about the time, energy, and cost of upkeep. I could see that gravel gardening offered them hope—a way to replace some lawn and create beautiful, resilient gardens without regularly applying chemicals and water, and without churning out more pollutants.

Sharing the Stories of Inspiring Gravel Gardens

Throughout my travels, I have discovered many nuances of gravel gardening—not just the techniques but the heartfelt stories behind them. While researching gardens for this book, writer Teresa Woodard and I met a host of talented and passionate gardeners and garden designers. Some were fairly new to gardening, like Mike Cunningham, who wanted a gravel garden to celebrate the life of his late wife. And then there were the young, eco-conscious students like Amiah, Sydney, and Tess at Stephen F. Austin State University in Texas, who learned firsthand from Dr. Jared Barnes the possibilities of this incredible method. We also spent time with professional gardeners that have taken the gravel gardening concept to new heights, like the incredibly artistic Lisa Roper at Chanticleer in Wayne, Pennsylvania, and horticulturist Avery Pronschinske at Olbrich Botanical Gardens in Madison, Wisconsin, who shares her passion and skills with Olbrich's 350,000 annual visitors. Ed Lyon's creative design of the Hillside Garden at Iowa State University's Reiman Gardens in Ames, Iowa, took us to new levels—literally. The sinuous, accessible path slowly ascends the steep hillside, revealing the inventive plantings and wonderful, borrowed views.

Along the way, we found that some gardeners just love to push the limits of what a garden can do and aren't happy unless they're trying new and interesting plants. Andrew Bunting and Glenn Ashton, gardeners extraordinaire, are both pushing the plant limits in the Philadelphia area, growing all sorts of cool succulents, cacti, and alpine gems that few thought could possibly grow there. And just a few states away in Tiverton, Rhode Island, garden designer and nurseryman Sean Conway is doing the same in his gravel garden, which was previously a high-maintenance vegetable garden he used as a TV set for his gardening show, *Cultivating Life*. Sean, an avid plant collector, was inspired by the work at Chatto and Chanticleer gardens, and now his artistic garden inspires others, including me.

We also saw gravel gardens as practical solutions for public spaces, like the City of Madison's transformation of a leaky fountain into a beautiful three-tiered gravel garden, or the striking parking lot islands they've created for easy upkeep. Swarthmore College's roundabout and parking islands were completely brought to life by Adam Glas and Jeff Jabco, who were inspired by Cassian's groundbreaking work in Germany. Photographer Bob Stefko and I never dodged so many cars on a photoshoot as we did when he captured Adam and his curb-bordered gardens. And Cassian himself shared his innovative work at Hermannshof and his collaborative urban greening projects with wife Bettina Jaugstetter.

We also found that gravel gardens can enhance lives in urban areas or offer respite when needed most. In Chicago, we visited gardens created by a dedicated and inspiring team that is bringing beauty to inner-city neighborhoods through its Adopt A Lot program. The greening project also provides training

and jobs for residents. In Dungeness, England, we paid homage to Derek Jarman's iconic seaside garden—a unique creative refuge for the gardener, artist, and activist while battling AIDS in the early '90s.

Some gardens we visited are rooted in a profound sense of place, like the prairie-inspired gravel garden of Ana McCracken in Ames, Iowa, crafted in collaboration with the talented Midwestern designer Kelly Norris. At Sissinghurst Castle in Kent, England, the Delos Garden was revitalized to reflect the vision of its founders, who fell in love with the landscape of a Greek island. And only 50 miles down the road, there is the amazing rewilding story of Knepp Castle in West Sussex, now home to more than a thousand grazing animals and in the heart of the estate a walled gravel garden that is teeming with life.

Not all gravel gardens are small, of course, and the business-campus gardens of Argonne National Laboratory in Lemont, Illinois, and Epic Systems in Verona, Wisconsin, are proof. These innovative businesses broke the molds of the classic corporate campus by setting examples of what others can do to invest in their employees and give back to our planet. When shooting the gardens at Epic in full autumn glory, it was hard to believe that we were standing atop an underground parking garage for 2100 vehicles.

And last, but certainly not least, we visit the GOAT of gravel gardening, Beth Chatto Gardens in Essex, England, where Beth's granddaughter Julia Boulton is now carrying the torch. We also see Beth's ideals through Julia's work at nearby Chattowood, a new residential community committed to eco-conscious gardens.

And then there's my own garden, here on a small residential street in Madison, Wisconsin, my home of twenty-three years. Beginning the book with my small garden allows us to take a closer look at the "nitty gritty" elements of gravel gardening.

My Wish

Whether you're an experienced gardener, a newcomer, or simply someone who appreciates beautiful gardens like my wife, Kathy, I hope you enjoy this book. If you want to create more beauty with less work, provide a haven for pollinators and other animals, or simply garden in a way that's kinder to the earth, I invite you to explore the possibilities of gravel gardening. And if you have a bit of space to spare, even a small one, give it a try—you may be surprised by the rewards and joy that gravel gardening can bring.

Jeff Epping

Gravel
at
Home

JEFF EPPING
Madison, Wisconsin

Gravel Garden Blueprint

My personal gravel garden came about a bit serendipitously. When we moved into our home the front lawn was completely full of Kentucky bluegrass, like every other home on the street. Environmentally speaking, I knew I could do better, so I tore it up and replaced it with a super drought-tolerant fine fescue seed mix. It was far from a traditional manicured lawn, and I tended it rather naturally, giving it little extra water and no fertilizer or other chemicals. Since I only mowed it in the fall, its fine-textured blades grew long and created swirling clumps and graceful undulating waves that gave it a fun, whimsical look. But when the city installed a new sewer line and had to destroy the lawn in 2017, I decided it was time to do something even better—something even less labor-intensive, and even more ecologically beneficial that was still beautiful for myself and my neighbors to enjoy.

At first, I considered a prairie garden like one I'd admired in a nearby neighborhood. However, I'd been working with gravel gardens for a few years on several projects and was really impressed with them. I came to appreciate how their essential layer of washed gravel made it tough for weed seeds to germinate and root in. A gravel garden would save me time—up to 80 percent less work, I discovered—and save resources with no annual mulching, little to no irrigation after the first year or two, and no mowing. Not to mention that I was impressed with their environmental benefits like feeding pollinators and birds, conserving water, and eliminating the need for fuel, herbicides, and fertilizers.

After thinking more about it, I became convinced that a gravel garden would be the perfect fit for our cottage-style home, tucked into the existing shrub and perennial borders. I decided to go with a shorter plant palette, keeping everything under 18 inches, with blooms that transitioned seamlessly from spring through fall. I needed the garden to be beautiful in more relatable, recognizable ways to get neighbors to accept what is ultimately a wilder-looking, naturalistic style. I envisioned a flower show starting with spring bulbs like glory-of-the-snow and ornamental onions followed by summer coneflowers and coreopsis, then closing out fall with asters, goldenrods, and textural grasses like prairie dropseed and little bluestem.

Once the bulldozers pulled out and the dust settled in the fall of 2017, I stripped what was left of the lawn, installed the stone edging, ordered the plants, and recruited our kids to help spread a 4- to 5-inch layer of gravel when they were home for spring break. As soon as spring arrived, the fun began—planting 225 small plants into the gravel. Once we were finished planting, I added "cues of care"—a whimsical metal sculpture near the front door, a Frank Lloyd Wright–inspired bee house, and pathways to the front door and side gate.

The first year, weeding was limited to the crowns of plants, germinating "bonus gift" seeds that popped up as I watered often to help the plants establish. By the second year, weeds were minimal, and the new plants were thriving with only one supplemental watering during a very dry period that summer. By the third year, the plants had fully filled in. Not much of the gravel showed other than in early spring, just an impressive meadow of flowering perennials and

OPPOSITE After working with gravel gardens for about ten years at Olbrich Botanical Gardens and Epic Systems, I decided it was high time to create one at my home. In 2017, the City of Madison gave me the perfect opportunity when they renovated my street and almost completely destroyed my existing front lawn.

Post-lawn, the gravel garden is the perfect solution for something less labor-intensive, more ecologically beneficial, and still beautiful for me and my neighbors. I wanted to create a garden that wasn't just for me to enjoy--I wanted a garden that would support all the creatures that lived in, or could live in, my neighborhood.

grasses and an abundance of pollinating bees and butterflies. If this sounds like a dream come true, well, it was.

Each fall, I further enhanced my gravel garden, planting colorful spring bulbs like ornamental onions, small-flowered daffodils, and species tulips. In 2021, I removed a pagoda dogwood and some Japanese yews near the house and expanded the gravel garden, adding a few larger plants like big bluestem, prairie dock, and showy milkweed.

Over the past eight years, I've had fun experimenting with different plants and learned some valuable lessons. First, I discovered that some plants tend to reseed along the curb where sand from snowplows and salt trucks accumulate. Keeping an eye on them in spring made it easy to pull the weeds, and occasionally I let some stay if they were species already thriving in the gravel garden. Second, I learned that certain plants, particularly purple prairie clover, are irresistible to rabbits and despite attempts to get them established, I finally had to give up. Voles posed another challenge. During one snowy winter, they happily burrowed under the snow and feasted on the crowns of prairie dropseed and the deep taproots of pale purple coneflower. Third, I found that some plants, like prairie baby's breath and tickseed, grew taller than I wanted in high-rainfall years. However, cutting them back by half in late spring helped keep their height more in scale with the rest of the garden later on. Another fun trick I tried was planting colorful annuals in 6-inch-long clay tiles I turned vertically and filled with soil. This allowed me to easily plant them without digging into the gravel each spring.

I witnessed firsthand how resilient gravel garden plants are, especially when they excelled during the droughts in 2023 and then again in 2024. While the plants were visibly shorter, they still performed beautifully without any supplemental watering. I also discovered I could grow things in the gravel garden that had previously failed in my perennial borders. Before, plants like lavender, German statice, and hairy penstemon would rot in winter, but now they are completely unfazed in the well-drained gravel garden.

Today, I'm very happy with the garden's beauty and ease of care, and proud of the fact that it is full of life. Perhaps the biggest joy comes from my neighbors' responses. No doubt they thought my idea was a little crazy at first. They now often stop while on walks with positive comments and questions. I love sharing the garden's story—pointing out butterflies and their favorite nectar plants, explaining how the gravel acts as a natural weed barrier, and offering advice on top plant choices for this style of gardening.

Two of my biggest fans have been my neighbor Katy and her dog, Frankie. When the garden was in full bloom, Katy often complimented other areas of my garden but never mentioned the gravel garden. One day, curious, I asked her directly: "Katy, what do you think of the gravel garden?"

She looked a little uncomfortable and reluctantly replied, "Honestly, it's a bit much."

Undaunted, I took a few minutes to explain that there's more behind this garden than other gardens that I simply planted for looks. For this one, I shared, I wanted to do something that was also good for the environment. I didn't want to run a mower or use harmful chemicals. I tried to make this point by showing her a prairie baby's breath brimming with happy pollen-covered insects.

"I love all the flowers; it's just a little unusual," she said before continuing her walk.

Two weeks later, I casually waved to Katy as I was getting the mail. She stopped and said, "I just wanted to tell you how much I appreciate your garden. Every time Frankie and I walk by, we now stop to see what bugs are on the flowers."

That moment reaffirmed my belief that many people, like Katy, want to embrace more eco-friendly gardens and gardening practices—they just need a little inspiration.

OPPOSITE I use my small home garden as a laboratory to test new design ideas and trial plants. Besides my gravel garden out front, I've planted a sedge meadow and other shade-loving perennials in my backyard among oak and birch trees, espaliered fruit trees alongside the house, and loaded my patio with containers filled with new perennials and a few annuals to observe up close.

Gravel Gardening Basics

CHOOSE A SITE. First, select a sunny, open site that has decent soil drainage. A dry, sunny spot along a driveway, sidewalk, south side of a home, or front curb is ideal. Next, remove any existing lawn or plantings, making sure to get rid of tenacious weeds with extensive root systems that may come back to haunt you later. This is typically done with a sod cutter, a smothering method often utilizing cardboard or plastic, or a nonselective herbicide like glyphosate. If there are existing drought-tolerant shrubs, they can be left in place and designed into the gravel garden. Just remove any loose soil, mulch, or other organic matter from around their crowns.

DIAGRAM A PLAN. Outline the shape of the space and note key measurements. Start a wish list of plants including grasses and perennials. Consider the plant height and strive for a palette of plants that offer a succession of blooms. For inspiration, review the plant galleries and accompanying plant descriptions included in many of the chapters throughout this book. Next, determine the square footage of the space to calculate the amount of gravel and plants needed. The internet is loaded with free gravel and plant calculators to help consumers out—all you need to do is plug in your numbers and they'll figure out amounts for you.

ABOVE For the gravel garden, I chose my front yard which is in full sun except for the shade of a couple of trees and along the driveway where conventional perennial beds are planted. The front had once been a traditional lawn (top left), then a fescue lawn (top right) before the city crews came in and tore up the lawn for a new sewer line and street (bottom left). I decided it was time for a gravel garden (bottom right).

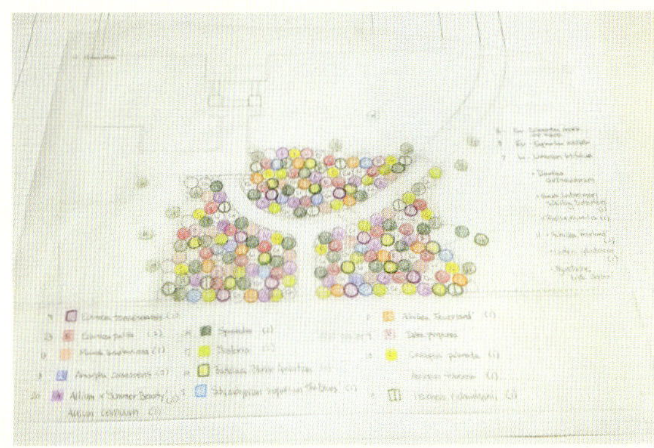

INSTALL AN EDGE. Enclose the space with a solid border or hard edge if one doesn't already exist. Medium stones, large boulders, or stacked pavers work well. The foundation of a building, a driveway, an existing sidewalk, or a concrete curb also make good edgers. Just be sure an edge surrounds the perimeter and is tall enough to retain a full 5 inches of gravel. This edge is critical because it retains the gravel at a consistent depth throughout the garden. If gravel tapers off at the edges, weeds will easily find their way into the soil below and germinate.

SPREAD THE GRAVEL. For the gravel layer, use washed ¼- to ⅜-inch quartzite or granite chip gravel for the best results. Avoid larger gravel that has bigger openings between each stone and allows organic matter to build up within the gravel layer, giving weed seeds favorable conditions for germination. Local gray angular quartzite or round pea gravel is ideal, but any stone of similar

TOP LEFT I made a simple plan on graph paper, so that I could easily draw it to scale and figure out the square footage of the space (550 square feet). This helped me calculate how much quartzite gravel to order for a 4- to 5-inch layer (11 to 12 tons) and how many plants I would need to fill the space (198). I was so impressed by the beauty and ease of care that I expanded the garden three years later. TOP RIGHT I kept all of the original soil and created a border around three sides of the garden. I dug in a combination of glacial boulders (unearthed by the street project) and locally sourced limestone pieces set on a diagonal for an artistic flair. The new concrete curb was a perfect edge along the street. All of the edging stones and curb are 6+ inches above the soil line, so they keep the gravel from spilling into adjacent beds or the street. BOTTOM ROW I drove stakes firmly into the soil, spaced about 3 feet apart, and marked them at 5 inches and 6 inches to make it easy to consistently spread the gravel at the correct depth. I was careful not to work any soil into the gravel when spreading it and slowly removed the stakes for the same reason.

size and hardness is fine. Every piece of gravel will be relatively the same size and remain loose, retaining the air space between them, much like marbles in a jar. If the planting bed is large, it's a good idea to drive in stakes about every 3 to 5 feet. Make a mark on the stakes about 5 inches above the soil line to help ensure a consistent depth of 4 to 5 inches while spreading the gravel. This is a very important detail because the gravel acts as a barrier to weed seed germination. Too deep, and the plants perform poorly. Too shallow, and weed seedlings will take hold in the soil below, establishing in your nice, clean gravel garden.

ADD THE PLANTS. First, select drought-tolerant, deep-rooting species ideally in 3½- to 4½-inch pots. These size pots typically hold plants with 4-inch root balls that can be molded to the depth of the gravel layer. Larger potted plants can be used, but the root balls will have to be reduced to match the depth of the gravel. This can be more difficult, costly, and time-consuming. Smaller pots or plugs can also be used, but they take longer to root in the soil, making them more vulnerable to drought stress as they get established. Plants are typically spaced anywhere from 12 inches to 16 inches on center, depending upon their mature sizes. Tighter-than-usual spacing is best. The goal is to cover the gravel with vegetation and create a living, interacting community of plants.

Before inserting plants, loosen tight roots if needed, and peel off the top ½ to 1 inch of soil mix to rid yourself of dormant weed seeds that will be sure to germinate later. Put this excess potting soil in a bucket—never mix it in with the gravel. Dig a hole in the gravel, taking care not to stir up the soil below the gravel. Insert the plant and cover the root ball with gravel, making sure the plant's crown is even or just below the surface of the gravel layer. Once the garden is planted, you will have a sea of gravel with a few dots of green here and there. Even though you see more gravel than plants in the first season or two, don't despair; that will quickly change as the plants grow to maturity. In two to three years, you will enjoy a beautiful tapestry of lush, colorful plants and the gravel will lie hidden below, doing its job of controlling your weeds.

OPPOSITE I followed my plan as I placed the pots on the gravel before planting (top left). This mock-up shows how the crown of the plant is even with the surface of the gravel, and the root ball is just touching the soil below the gravel layer (bottom left). When preparing the root ball for planting, it's important to catch all of the soil so it doesn't contaminate the clean gravel (bottom right). I wanted to plug in some drought-tolerant annuals for consistent color, so I cut clay drain tiles to 6- to 8-inch lengths, buried them in the gravel, and filled them with soil (top right). The annual plugs are easy to plant, and their roots spread in the soil below the gravel.

ABOVE, LEFT TO RIGHT (a) I like smaller potted plants (quarts are ideal) for ease of transplanting and cost savings. (b) Remove the pot and peel off the top inch of soil where weed seeds lay dormant--all soil goes in a bucket. (c) Loosen roots and mold the ball to about 5 inches in length. (d) By hand, remove gravel down to the soil. (e) Place the plant in the hole with the roots in contact with the soil below. (f) Fill the gravel back around the root ball.

ESTABLISH AND CARE FOR THE GARDEN. Establishing your plants is very different in a gravel bed than in a conventional perennial bed or border. Maintenance will be much easier in the long run, but getting the garden off to a good start is a time commitment and critical to its long-term success. The key to a good start is water, water, and more water. This seems contrary to the whole gravel garden concept, which is about gardening with less water, but the water requirement changes as the plants root in. Once they reach maturity, they will, in turn, reach their maximum drought tolerance. Even though the plant species selected for the garden are naturally drought-tolerant, they need to root deeply into the soil below the gravel before they can go without supplemental water. It's important to start them out strong, giving them the tools they need to thrive later.

Keep in mind that the only moisture available to the plant initially is in the soil mass that it was planted with; the surrounding gravel has little to no water-holding capacity. Water the plants as if they were still in the plastic pots that they were initially grown in. In the beginning, that may mean daily watering on sunny, hot, windy days. As the plants grow and root in, the watering will become less frequent. The best way to know when it's time to water is by monitoring the plants each morning. Water when you see signs of stress—most often, off-colored and wilting foliage. A good way to make it easy on yourself and your plants is to set up a temporary irrigation system that can be left in place for the first season. Hoses and impact sprinklers are relatively inexpensive and worth the investment. Water by hand whenever possible to conserve this precious resource, but when it's not possible, the sprinklers do a good job of quenching plants' thirst.

ABOVE The new plants are planted in a sea of gravel and need to be watered daily at first, then less as their roots grow deeper and wider and draw available water in the soil. While small gardens are easily hand-watered, temporary irrigation systems may be useful for larger gardens. Watering (top left and right) won't be necessary after the plants are established in two to three years (bottom left and right). Weeding is minimal and is only needed when plants seed along edges of pathways where organic matter builds up or in the crowns of existing plants. Most of the self-seeders are plants that are already in the garden due to their drought tolerance--some you may want to keep.

ABOVE Spring cleanup is extremely important--organic-matter buildup in the gravel will render it useless in keeping weed seeds from getting established in the garden. Depending upon the year, I usually cut back my garden in mid- to late March to early April--prior to bulb emergence and new plant growth. Recent research has shown that cutting stems to about 12 to 18 inches and leaving them standing in the garden is beneficial to stem-nesting insects. I remove the remainder of the plant parts and cut longer stems to 18- to 24-inch lengths, and move them to other areas of my garden, inconspicuously tucking them behind shrubs where any hibernating insects or egg masses can emerge naturally. The plants slowly break down and contribute to the health of the soil (top left). I carefully remove sand-laden ice sheets and leaves along the road edge as soon as possible in spring (top right). Tools are minimal, and only hand pruners, rake, and tarp are needed for the bulk of the cleanup (middle left and right). A day or two after the initial cleanup, giving the gravel time to dry, I use my battery-powered blower (bottom left) to remove any last bits and pieces of organic matter. The garden is now ready for the season ahead (bottom right).

Personal Favorites

❶ **Butterfly milkweed** (*Asclepias tuberosa*). Few plant species are as well adapted to gravel gardens and provide as much aesthetic appeal and ecological function as this amazing plant. ❷ **Lanceleaf coreopsis** (*Coreopsis lanceolata*) offers bright cheery flowers for nearly three months and then produces seeds for many songbirds like goldfinches to feast on later in the season. ❸ **Wild quinine** (*Parthenium integrifolium*) is a gravel garden stalwart with attractive white flowers clustered in cauliflower-like heads that dry in late summer and remain attractive through winter. ❹ **Prairie sedge** (*Carex brevior*) is not as well-known as other sedges, but it should be for its clean dark green foliage and airy spring flower heads that provide seed for sparrows and other songbirds. ❺ **'Summer Beauty' ornamental onion** (*Allium lusitanicum* 'Summer Beauty') has been around for quite some time and still remains one of the best cultivars of ornamental onions, with clean medium-green foliage and gorgeous, pink, golf-ball-sized flower heads that are always loaded with pollinators.

❻ **Autumn moor grass** (*Sesleria autumnalis*) is a very drought-tolerant, cool-season grass with fresh, limey-green leaves that come up early in the season and send up silvery seed heads in autumn. They sparkle in the evening fall sun, then later turn dark brown and contrast beautifully against the lighter foliage. ❼ **'Dark Towers' beardtongue** (*Penstemon* 'Dark Towers') is one of the first perennials to bloom in the gravel garden in May. Its lavender-pink flowers are stunning against the wine-purple foliage. The purple seed heads carry the show for the remainder of the season. ❽ **Calamint** (*Calamintha nepeta* ssp. *nepeta*) is probably the longest-blooming perennial in the gravel garden. Its frothy white bottlebrush flower heads look good with every plant around them up until a killing frost. This subspecies is sterile and won't become a weed like the straight species can. ❾ **Tennessee coneflower** (*Echinacea tennesseensis*) is one of the top-performing coneflowers in the gravel garden, renowned for its longevity and beautiful floral displays in the heat of summer.

RIGHT The gravel layer allows me to grow a host of fun, curb-appealing, drought-tolerant plants including cliff goldenrod (*Solidago drummondii*), calamint (*Calamintha nepeta* ssp. *nepeta*), 'Feuerland' yarrow (*Achillea* 'Feuerland'), and the nearly everblooming gold-flowered yellow corydalis (*Corydalis lutea*) that often seeds into the crowns of neighboring plants but is very easily removed if unwanted. **BELOW RIGHT** Carthusian pink (*Dianthus carthusianorum*), unlike other related species, is tall and airy in the garden and is drought-tolerant enough to occasionally self-sow in the pure gravel between plants.

LEFT I thoughtfully place art throughout the garden as "cues for care," like these rusted metal fiddleheads that I made.

I've learned a few tricks. In wetter years, when some of my plants grew taller than desired, I experimented the next season by giving them the "Chelsea chop"--cutting them back by half in late spring. The native flowering spurge (*Euphorbia corollata*) and tickseed (*Coreopsis palmata*) responded beautifully with short strong stems and colorful flowers, as did yellow corydalis (*Corydalis lutea*). I'm also trialing various bulbs that require good drainage, like kniphofias, fritillaries, and foxtail lilies.

My garden supports a wealth of wildlife from a host of insect species to many songbirds that feed them to their young and feast on the garden's seeds. Small mammals like deer-footed mice, chipmunks, flying and gray squirrels, and rabbits traverse the garden. I occasionally see predators like sharp-shinned hawks, owls, and foxes that need them to survive. I built a wooden bee house for the many resident solitary bees, which also makes a nice garden ornament.

Today, I delight in the garden's beauty and the lightened workload, but first and foremost, the satisfaction that my garden is contributing to the healing of our planet. I'm also happy to share that home landscapes don't need to have traditional lawns and all the environmentally damaging baggage that comes with them. I'm convinced that in due time, more people will embrace eco-conscious gardens and gardening techniques of all kinds, including gravel gardens.

ANA and ED MCCRACKEN with KELLY NORRIS
Ames, Iowa

Prairie-Inspired Garden with a Sense of Place

At age 59, writer and MFA candidate Ana McCracken enrolled in a western history class about the Great Plains at Iowa State University. Her heart ached as she learned about the Dust Bowl, a stark reminder of the ecological devastation brought by human actions.

"It made me sad to learn an entire ecosystem was ploughed under," she says and was moved to restore a patch of her own prairie.

The opportunity came when she and her husband, Ed, purchased a neighboring lot to their Ames, Iowa, home. The addition restored their property to its original 1-acre size, creating a prominent corner across from Iowa State University Alumni Center.

"This is my ode to prairie," says Ana. Her vision was a prairie garden brimming with native plants to attract pollinators and insects for birds, requiring minimal water and inspiring others to embrace a more naturalistic landscaping style.

Enter Kelly Norris, an Iowa State University alumnus and champion for naturalistic garden design.

Upon arrival, Kelly found a bare lot with compacted soil, a challenge he embraced.

"He was so excited about the sandy, gravely soil," says Ana. "He wouldn't even let our contractor bring in topsoil."

Kelly told them, "This is actually exactly what we want," and shared his vision to create a gravel garden replicating Iowa's ridge prairies found on similar gravely soil.

"The magic is in the till," he told them.

The gravel garden approach ended up a winning solution on multiple counts. It worked with the existing infertile soil. It embraced a sense of place by mimicking the region's prairies. And it offered low-maintenance upkeep—ideal for a beginner gardener like Ana.

The key was to incorporate plenty of natural beauty and curb appeal. The McCrackens were especially mindful of recent city ordinances regarding overgrown "eco-friendly" gardens. Kelly addressed this public concern by incorporating design elements that signaled care such as year-round interest, formal evergreen accents, and steel-edged paths.

His immersive design featured winding paths through a series of raised oval-shaped beds. These "mini drumlins," Kelly explained, mimicked the oval landforms of glacial till left behind by ancient glaciers. No surprise, place genius is a signature of Kelly's designs.

"I'm in love with place," he says. "As a way to ground projects, I always like to grab something of local interest that's unique to the place."

Around these unique drumlins, Kelly deliberately expanded and contracted the pathways to encourage visitors to pause as they moved through the plantings.

He assembled two plant palettes, catering to Ana's love of golden summer blooms and warm fall colors and textures.

"Fall and winter are my favorite times of year," she says. "Kelly did a great job curating the garden

OPPOSITE After studying the Dust Bowl's devastating history in her master's program, writer Ana McCracken was inspired to create an "ode to prairie" on the side lot of her home near Iowa State University.

Ana and her husband, Ed, live on a prominent, 1-acre corner by the university's alumni center, so aesthetics count. The garden was designed with plenty of curb appeal, including elements like showy plants with year-round interest, formal evergreen accents, and steel-edged paths. Yellow-flowering prairie dock even bends to welcome passersby.

with regionally native plants with a rolling seasonality of color and interest."

The first taller plant palette envelops the site with selections occasionally repeated in the middle for continuity. Among these taller plant selections are 'Holy Smoke' big bluestem, Golden Sunset® yellow prairie grass, and rattlesnake master. The second shorter palette features native plants from the region's dry hilltop prairies. Kelly filled the mini drumlins with a mix of grasses—'Honeycomb' blue grama grass, 'Standing Ovation' and 'Twilight Zone' little bluestems, and 'Golden Prairie' prairie dropseed—then accented them with bursts of color from 'Floristan White' blazing star, black-eyed Susan, and upright prairie coneflowers.

Privacy borders along the edges of the gravel garden were defined with 'Taylor' eastern red cedars, and regionally adapted quaking aspens.

Fall of 2021 marked the garden's installation. Kelly collaborated with Iowa State classmate Ben Hershey of Country Landscapes in Ames. Ben's team started by manually breaking up the existing compacted sandy loam, mounding soil to form the raised drumlins, then edging them in Corten steel. Next, they sourced 1/4- to 1/2-inch washed pea gravel from a local quarry and spread it in a 5-inch layer across the narrow lot. Within this gravel layer, they planted more than 3700 plants, then watered them periodically as needed until first frost.

Today, the garden is a low-maintenance haven for the McCrackens and a delight for passersby. Summer boasts drifts of yellow flowers and white spires dotted among a layer of grasses. Fall transforms the scene with rich purple, brown, and red grasses, accented by the silhouettes of rounded seed heads and lingering umbels. Ana's connection to the garden has deepened over time. Once a novice, she's become a steward, marveling at pollinators the garden attracts and frequently consulting Kelly for plant identification.

"I basically weed and that's all, thanks to the gravel layer," says Ana. "I don't need to water."

A writer at heart, Ana plans to add educational signage and plant labels this year, sharing the garden's story and inspiring others to embrace the beauty and benefits of naturalistic gardens.

"I want to share it with others and be a champion for these gardens," she says.

For Ana, this curated prairie transcends aesthetics. With ancestral roots in northern Minnesota, Ana was adopted in California and later raised in Illinois. She returned to Ames and her Midwestern roots late in life. The garden, a miniature reflection of the Great Plains prairies, provides a sense of belonging and peace.

"It allows me to breathe and exhale," she says. "I am home."

ABOVE The cool white orbs of rattlesnake master float above the brilliant gold flowers of black-eyed Susan. OPPOSITE For the garden's design, Ana turned to Kelly Norris, an Iowa State University alumnus and champion for naturalistic garden design. She shared with him her vision--a prairie garden brimming with native plants to attract pollinators and insects for birds, requiring minimal water and inspiring others to embrace a more naturalistic landscaping style.

Cues for Care: Curating the Gravel Garden Aesthetic

Appearances count when it comes to building support for gravel gardens and other naturalistic-style landscapes. Joan Nassauer, a professor of landscape architecture at the University of Michigan School for Environment and Sustainability, coined the phrase "cues to care" to sum up her landscape strategy in her article "Messy Ecosystems, Orderly Frames" (*Landscape Journal*, fall 1995). She argues that our society has expectations to display care in landscapes, and by using recognizable design features, like curved paths or stone edges, garden designers can build community acceptance for "messy, wilder" naturalistic designs. Here are some simple strategies to show cues for care:

PATCHES OF LAWN: Mow a strip of lawn along a narrow meadow or leave a circle of lawn within a naturalistic planting as a familiar design component and resting place for the eye.

EDGING: Line wilder plantings with stone or metal edging to add definition.

GARDEN ART: Place sculptures within naturalistic landscapes to signal the plantings are intentional.

FORMAL EVERGREEN: Install columnar evergreens like 'Taylor' eastern red cedars to add recognizable structure to wilder plantings.

PATHS: Carve paths of stone, brick, or gravel through naturalistic gardens to create another welcoming design element.

GARDEN WALLS: Use natural hedging or stone walls to enclose abundant plantings, creating "orderly frames" and intimate garden rooms.

DECORATIVE FENCE: Add iron or wooden fencing to define boundaries and suggest enclosure, even if still publicly visible.

COLORFUL FLOWERS: Plant swaths of bold, flowering natives within meadow plantings for plenty of curb appeal. Layer plants with varying bloom times for a succession of colors.

SEATING: Strategically place benches or seating areas within naturalistic gardens as an inviting design element.

TIDINESS: Cut a neat edge along a naturalistic planting or selectively trim back flopping plants to show a landscape is cared for.

EDUCATIONAL SIGNAGE: Add signage to inform passersby about the garden's ecological purpose, its native plants and the wildlife it supports. The National Wildlife Federation and Doug Tallamy's Homegrown National Park offer signage for certified wildlife habitats.

ABOVE Swaths of bold, flowering natives add plenty of visual appeal. Layering plants with varying heights, textures, foliage, flower colors, and successive blooms creates a beautiful garden that brims with life.

'Taylor' eastern red cedar (*Juniperus virginiana* 'Taylor') with its narrow columnar form adds recognizable structure to the wilder-looking plantings.

Prairie Standouts

❶ **Butterfly milkweed** (*Asclepias tuberosa*) and its bright orange flowers pop in the summer garden and provide food for both the caterpillars and adult butterflies of the coveted monarch butterfly. ❷ **Whorled milkweed** (*Asclepias verticillata*) is a lesser-known species of milkweed that is equally important to monarchs and beautiful in the garden. Its finer texture and bright white flowers give way to slender pods that split in fall and release delightful seed silks that float off in the wind. ❸ **Mexican hat** (*Ratibida columnifera*) grows best in dry infertile soils like in its native habitat, so it is right at home in the gravel garden. ❹ **'Sweet as Honey' black-eyed Susan** (*Rudbeckia* × 'Sweet as Honey') is one of Kelly's favorite cultivars for its less formal look and exceptional performance in the garden. Finer-textured, disease-resistant foliage and daintier flowers on long, upright stems give it a lighter presence and sense of belonging in a naturalistic planting. ❺ **Locally sourced gravels:** Washed pea gravel (¼- to ½-inch-size) was spread 5 inches deep in the planting beds and contrasts nicely with the dark gray ¾-inch limestone trap rock in the paths. ❻ **'Twilight' aster** (*Eurybia* × *herveyi* 'Twilight') grows well in a shadier pocket of the gravel garden. Its near-blue flowers with yellow eyes are borne in profusion in late summer and fall. ❼ **'Honeycomb' blue grama grass** (*Bouteloua gracilis* 'Honeycomb') is prized for its delicate seed heads and proven to be a hardier cultivar than the popular 'Blonde Ambition' for Midwestern gardens. ❽ **'Midnight Oil' eastern bee balm** (*Monarda bradburiana* 'Midnight Oil') is a beautiful disease-resistant cultivar with deep green glossy foliage, light pink flowers in early spring, and button-shaped seed heads that last through fall and winter.

BELOW The native and intensely colorful milkweed bugs have coevolved with our native milkweeds and even migrate south for the winter like monarchs do. Leave them be, and enjoy their beauty as you would colorful flowers in your garden.

ABOVE Quaking aspens (*Populus tremuloides*) were planted to add height to the garden, as well as for their beautiful bark that is especially nice in winter. The sound of the leaves quaking in the wind is delightful on a breezy day. **RIGHT** Kelly filled the drumlins with a mix of grasses--'Honeycomb' blue grama, 'Standing Ovation' and 'Twilight Zone' little bluestems, and 'Golden Prairie' prairie dropseed--then accented them with bursts of color from 'Floristan White' blazing stars, black-eyed Susan, and the towering prairie dock.

ABOVE Ana's connection to the garden has deepened over time. Once a novice, she's become a steward, marveling at pollinators the garden attracts and having fun learning about all the plants. **RIGHT** Kelly's immersive design features winding paths through a series of raised oval-shaped beds. These mini drumlins mimic the oval landforms of glacial till left behind by ancient glaciers. **OPPOSITE** Kelly assembled two plant palettes, catering to Ana's love of golden summer blooms and warm fall colors and textures. A taller plant palette (top row) envelops the site with 'Holy Smoke' big bluestem, Golden Sunset® yellow prairie grass, and rattlesnake master. The second, shorter palette features native plants like spotted bee balm (*Monarda punctata*) from the region's dry hilltop prairies (lower left).

Wildlife abounds in Ana's garden. Pictured here are a sulphur butterfly on calamint, brown-belted bumblebees on nodding onion, a bumblebee on rattlesnake master, and a monarch butterfly on an aptly named 'Butterfly Magnet' meadow blazing star. **OPPOSITE** Rattlesnake master (*Eryngium yuccifolium*) gracefully intertwines with 'Holy Smoke' big bluestem (*Andropogon gerardii* 'Holy Smoke').

Today, the garden is a low-maintenance haven for the McCrackens and a delight for passersby. Summer boasts drifts of yellow flowers with white and purple spires dotted among layers of grasses.

MIKE CUNNINGHAM
Madison, Wisconsin

Spouse's Loving Tribute

Mike Cunningham dreamed of a naturalistic garden to honor his late wife, Linda, an avid gardener and nature lover. Mike wasn't much of a gardener himself, but he was determined to create something beautiful and meaningful in her memory.

After Jeff Epping gave a talk at Olbrich Botanical Gardens in 2022, Mike learned about gravel gardens. He was impressed by their environmental benefits and low maintenance and saw how Jeff had designed and cared for them at Olbrich. Mike struck up a conversation with Jeff, sharing his desire for a garden that was both naturalistic and manageable.

"Originally, I was thinking of replacing the lawn with a lot of prairie grasses that I love, and only hoped I could keep out all the weeds," says Mike. Now, after Jeff's presentation, the gravel garden approach seemed the perfect fit.

At the end of their conversation, Mike asked Jeff to serve as project architect. Jeff was all in until he discovered Mike lived in a neighborhood with strict landscape rules. Nevertheless, Jeff agreed to serve with one caveat.

"Okay, here's the deal," he told Mike. "The first thing we need to do is talk to the HOA and see if they will approve this, because the last thing in the world we want is to install the garden and have it torn right out."

Undeterred, Mike delved into the HOA's bylaws, committed to gain board approval for his gravel garden. Mike's initial request was to replace all the lawn, and the response was an "absolute no." His neighborhood, built during the housing boom of 2007, was typical of many—closely spaced houses, uniform lawns, and shared amenities. Affordability and community were the cornerstones, reflected in the HOA's guidelines.

However, as Jeff and Mike more closely studied the seemingly rigid bylaws, they discovered some wiggle room.

"There's nothing on here that we can't satisfy," says Jeff who proceeded to create a beautiful plan for a naturalistic garden for Mike, all while complying with HOA guidelines. Jeff made small concessions like leaving a 3-foot strip of lawn along the perimeters and avoided planting in the common area between the sidewalk and street (also known as a "hell strip").

With the plan outline in place, Mike and Jeff began selecting plants. Jeff provided a comprehensive list, which Mike narrowed down to include his favorite native grasses and perennials. His top choices were switch grass, little bluestem, prairie dropseed, and grama grass. He also chose coneflowers, ornamental onions, amsonia, butterfly milkweed, false indigo, bee balm, beardtongue, Russian sage, black-eyed Susan, asters, goldenrod, and ironweed. Jeff also found a unique gold and yellow yucca (*Yucca filamentosa* 'Color Guard'), a familiar element from one of Linda's past gardens which serves as a living sculpture in this garden.

Next came the task of hiring a landscape contractor, and Mike had a local company in mind. The contractor was new to gravel gardens, so Jeff invited him to his home for a firsthand look at his own gravel garden. He was enthusiastic and reported a crew member was equally excited about the project.

OPPOSITE Mike Cunningham worked with Jeff Epping to design a naturalistic gravel garden to honor his late wife, Linda, an avid gardener and nature lover. Mike wasn't much of a gardener himself, so the gravel approach was a good, low-care fit.

530

Jeff worked within the HOA's guidelines to create a beautiful garden that neighbors now appreciate.

To prepare the site, the contractor's crew carefully followed Jeff's instructions. They removed 80 percent of the existing lawn, used a power rake to break up the base soil, created 1600 square feet of deep, curved beds along the front and side of the house, then lined them with 160 feet of stone edging. Two truckloads carrying 32 tons of quartzite gravel were brought in and spread to a depth of 5 inches within the defined stone borders. Naturally, the flurry of activity sparked mixed reactions among neighbors—some curious and others skeptical.

Finally, planting day arrived. The crew planted nearly 900 plants, each spaced a foot apart through the beds of gravel. Temporary sprinklers were set up with timers for the initial year's watering. By fall, the rains increased, so watering became unnecessary. Mike diligently kept an eye out for weeds—primarily thistles and dandelions which were present in the previous garden—and promptly removed any that appeared. By fall, the garden was flourishing.

The following spring, Mike was pleasantly surprised by the simple garden cleanup.

"I planned on a week or two of work, but it was far easier than I expected," he says, noting the cutback and cleanup was finished in a single day.

Today, Mike enjoys the beauty as much as the low maintenance of this commemorative garden which he lovingly named the Linda Valentine Memorial Garden.

"The gravel garden is an extraordinary concept," he says. "There's no place for weeds to root; it's beautiful, requires minimal water, no chemicals, and the birds and insects love it."

The garden has also garnered support from neighbors and attention from passersby. One cyclist, completely captivated, stopped abruptly and turned back to express his thanks and admiration to Mike for creating such a beautiful oasis in a sea of lawns.

Jeff wholeheartedly believes Mike is a natural steward for the garden. "Mike is caring for the garden like a seasoned pro," he says. "No doubt, Linda is smiling as she looks upon the garden that he made for her!"

ABOVE Jeff found a unique gold and yellow variegated yucca (*Yucca filamentosa* 'Color Guard'), one of Linda's favorite plants that Mike wanted to plant as a living sculpture in the garden. OPPOSITE Mike enjoys the beauty as much as the low maintenance of this commemorative garden, which he's lovingly named the Linda Valentine Memorial Garden. "The gravel garden is an extraordinary concept," he says. "There's no place for weeds to root; it's beautiful, requires minimal water, no chemicals, and the birds and insects love it."

Finding Common Ground with Your Homeowners Association

Creating a beautiful and sustainable garden doesn't have to clash with HOA regulations. Here are some tips to help you work with your HOA and achieve your goals:

KNOW THE RULES. Start by familiarizing yourself with the HOA's landscaping guidelines. Look for opportunities to incorporate naturalistic elements within the existing framework. For example, required foundation plantings can be transformed into gravel gardens with native plants. Also, take note of plant height restrictions. There are plenty of shorter native and regionally appropriate plants.

BEND A LITTLE. Sometimes, a few traditional touches can bridge the gap between a naturalistic design and HOA expectations. Consider a stone path or edging to define the space or incorporate a small patch of lawn.

TAP NEIGHBOR POWER. Enlist the support of your neighbors! Talk with them about your goals, whether you're attracting pollinators, reducing water usage, or simply creating a less maintenance-intensive space. Share pictures of beautiful, finished gravel gardens to help them visualize the positive outcome. Neighborly support goes a long way in preventing complaints and promoting your project within the community.

RECRUIT EXPERT HELP. If needed, seek support from a local environmental organization, a landscape architect, or watershed association. These experts can speak to the HOA board about the benefits of naturalistic gardens, such as preserving precious water and increasing plant biodiversity for pollinators and birds.

CELEBRATE SUCCESS. Once the garden is established, host a tour for your neighbors or local garden clubs. This is a great way to showcase the beauty and functionality of your design, and it can inspire others to consider similar projects.

CHANGE THE RULES. There is a national trend to have HOA rules changed to reflect our current climate challenges and protect our environment. If you face continued resistance, consider running for a position on the HOA board to advocate for change. You can also seek media coverage or support from the broader community to raise awareness about the benefits of naturalistic gardens. In some cases, working with elected officials can lead to legislation that allows HOA residents to plant these gardens and restricts HOAs from mandating turfgrass.

By following these tips and fostering a spirit of collaboration, you can create a beautiful, sustainable garden that benefits your home, your community, and the planet—all within the framework of your HOA.

ABOVE Leaving a little strip of mown lawn and creating "an orderly frame" with native limestone cobbles is not only functionally necessary for the garden, but important in showing a cue to care, as coined by renowned landscape architect Joan Nassauer. In her studies, she has found that people are more willing to accept the wildness of naturalistic plantings if they appear to be well tended. The garden has been well received by neighbors and passersby.

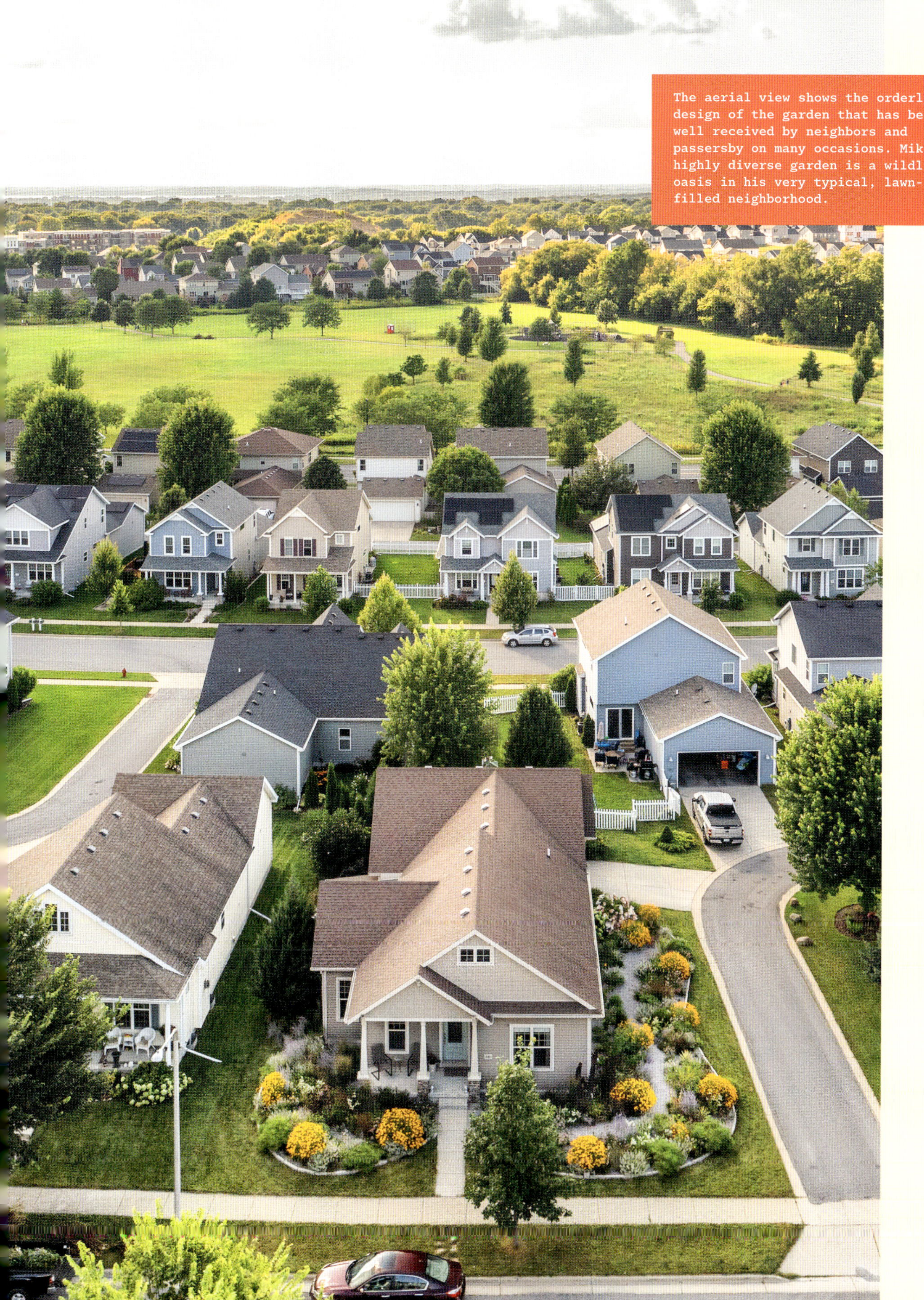

The aerial view shows the orderly design of the garden that has been well received by neighbors and passersby on many occasions. Mike's highly diverse garden is a wildlife oasis in his very typical, lawn-filled neighborhood.

Curbside Charmers

❶ **'Limelight' panicle hydrangea** (*Hydrangea paniculata* 'Limelight') existed in the garden and effectively hides an air-conditioning unit, so it was left in place, with the gravel garden built around it. ❷ **'Shenandoah' switch grass** (*Panicum virgatum* 'Shenandoah') is a nice dwarf cultivar of our native prairie grass, whose bluish-green blades take on brilliant red tones in summer and progress to burgundy by fall. It is most colorful and upright in form when grown in full sun. ❸ **Winecraft Black® smokebush** (*Cotinus coggygria* 'NCC01', Winecraft Black®) is well adapted to grow in the gravel garden, thriving in dry, hot conditions. This dwarf, dark burgundy–foliaged cultivar will reach about 6 feet at maturity and produce pink, smokelike flowers and seed heads. ❹ **Wild senna** (*Senna hebecarpa*) is another great native species that produces butter-yellow flower clusters atop 6-foot-tall stems that are clothed in finely divided compound foliage. Its foliage is a larval host to several species of sulphur and skipper butterflies. Its whimsical woody stems look great in winter. ❺ The pleasing color of the silvery-gray quartzite gravel blends nicely with its surroundings. The main job of the gravel is to deter weed invasion. The ⅜-inch washed chips spread 5 to 6 inches deep and hold no free moisture, making it very difficult for a seed to germinate—and if one does during a rainy spell, it is very hard for it to become established. ❻ **PowWow® Wild Berry coneflower** (*Echinacea purpurea* 'PAS702917', PowWow® Wild Berry) is a compact cultivar with intense, reddish-purple ray flowers around dark rose coneflowers. Though beautiful, *Echinacea purpurea* typically doesn't last as long in gravel gardens as some of its more drought-tolerant cousins like *E. pallida* and *E. tennesseensis*. ❼ **'Little Spire' Russian sage** (*Perovskia atriplicifolia* 'Little Spire') is an excellent upright compact cultivar that reaches just 18 to 24 inches tall and wide—about half the size of the naturally occurring species. ❽ **'Northwind' switch grass** (*Panicum virgatum* 'Northwind'), a tried-and-true, blue-green-foliaged cultivar discovered and introduced by Roy Diblik, is a strong upright cultivar of our native prairie grass. ❾ **'October Skies' aromatic aster** (*Symphyotrichum oblongifolium* 'October Skies') is a late-fall-blooming aster, sporting violet-blue ray petals with gold centers. Asters are often difficult to grow in gardens with heavy rabbit pressure, but this species' fragrant foliage is unpalatable to them and deer.

LEFT 'Little Spire' Russian sage (*Perovskia atriplicifolia* 'Little Spire') and calamint (*Calamintha nepeta* ssp. *nepeta*) welcome pollinators in the garden. This form of calamint is a seedless subspecies, which is significant since the wild form reseeds to the point of becoming a weed in gardens. **BELOW** Mike selected his favorite native grasses and perennials, including switch grass, little bluestem, prairie dropseed, and grama grass. He also chose coneflowers, amsonia, ornamental onion, butterfly milkweed, false indigo, bee balm, beardtongue, Russian sage, black-eyed Susan, aster, goldenrod, and ironweed. It's hard to believe that the garden has filled in this much in just one year.

The garden has been well accepted--something Mike and Jeff worried might not happen. One passing cyclist, completely captivated, stopped abruptly and turned back to express his thanks and admiration to Mike for creating such a beautiful oasis in a sea of lawns. ABOVE The luminescent blossoms of Tennessee coneflower (*Echinacea tennessensis*) demonstrate heliotropism, a botanical phenomenon where plants follow the sun throughout the day. OPPOSITE The rich golden flowers of black-eyed Susan (*Rudbeckia fulgida* 'Blovi', VIETTE'S LITTLE SUZY) glow in the afternoon sun and guide the eye down the welcoming gravel path.

Beyond beauty, the garden delights with the wildlife it supports, from butterflies and bunnies to beautiful great black wasps. The majority of wasps, like this great black wasp, are beneficial and not interested in harming humans. For more information on bees, wasps, and other pollinators, visit biologist Heather Holm's website at www.pollinatorsnativeplants.com. ABOVE The bold burgundy foliage of 'Dark Towers' beardtongue (*Penstemon* 'Dark Towers') contrasts beautifully in both color and texture to the lime-green, needle-leaved blue star (*Amsonia hubrichtii*).

Jeff loves how excited Mike is about his garden and wholeheartedly believes he's a natural steward. "Mike is caring for the garden like a seasoned pro," he says. "No doubt, Linda is smiling as she looks upon the garden that he made for her!"

The contractor removed 80 percent of the existing lawn, used a power rake to break up the base soil, and created 1600 square feet of deep, curved beds along the front and side of the house, then lined them with 160 feet of stone edging. Two truckloads carrying 32 tons of quartzite gravel were brought in and spread to a depth of 5 inches within the defined stone borders. Jeff and the crew finished the project, installing nearly 900 plants.

ANDREW BUNTING
Swarthmore, Pennsylvania

Plantsman's New Palette

In Swarthmore, Pennsylvania, a charming stone cottage overlooks rivers of gravel dotted with seasonal agaves and prickly pear cactus, soaring yucca, silvery mounds of catmint, and majestic plumes of moor grasses. For plantsman Andrew Bunting, this brave experimental gravel garden is the perfect laboratory to try out beloved, arid plants from around the world.

"It's a fun place to play around with a whole new palette of plants I haven't grown before," he says with delight.

As vice president of horticulture at the Pennsylvania Horticultural Society, Andrew tracks garden trends and eagerly adopts new styles both at work and home. Gravel gardens kept popping up on his radar as he traveled. He first discovered them at Beth Chatto's converted parking lot in Essex, England. Later, he was inspired by gravel garden designs in Pennsylvania at Swarthmore College's Scott Arboretum in Swarthmore and Chanticleer Garden in Wayne. He also experimented with them at Chicago Botanic Garden. There, he met Jeff Epping and studied his gravel projects at Olbrich Botanical Gardens and other gardens nearby.

Like many homebound gardeners during COVID, Andrew jumped at the chance to try a new garden project. Over the twenty-five years he's gardened at his home called "Belvidere," he's packed in varying garden types on the ⅓-acre property. He created broad perennial borders in the back and lined the patio with favorite tropical plants. He planted a woodland garden in the shade and carved out a vegetable garden in a sunny patch. He created a cottage-style meadow in front. When it became overgrown, he decided to transform the space into a new gravel garden.

"It had turned into a meadowy jungle and was ready for a change," says Andrew. During his four-year stint in Chicago, invasive weeds like lesser celandine, creeping buttercup, and star-of-Bethlehem had taken over the meadow and were difficult to eradicate.

"I had been impressed with other gravel gardens and decided to start my own," he said, explaining that he looked at it as an opportunity to grow different plants in a more xeriscape, arid or desert-esque, environment. The astute plantsman started assembling a plant list—drought-tolerant natives like ironweed and asters; tough perennials like alliums, lavenders, and spurges; and hardy cacti and succulents. He also set aside a few existing plants including three Hubricht's bluestars, three 'Skyracer' moor grasses, a chokeberry, a beautyberry, and three junipers.

To prepare the site, he called Bill Conwell, a local landscaper. Bill removed the top 6-inch layer of soil. Andrew's objective was to create a harsh environment for these tough plants while also eliminating his weed problem. The only elements left were the main stone walkway and a swath of lawn. Next, Bill and his team added 2 inches of gravel and rototilled it into the subsoil. They spread another 4 inches of ⅜-inch irregular granite gravel on top.

"It was a big sea of gravel," says Andrew, noting swaths extended from the front sidewalk, along both sides of a central stone walkway, around two patches of lawn, and all the way to a stone wall at the front of the house.

Now ready to plant, Andrew removed the plants from pots—many in gallon-size containers—then teased off the soil before planting them deep enough

OPPOSITE For plantsman Andrew Bunting, his bold experimental gravel garden is the perfect laboratory to try out beloved, arid plants from around the world.

Andrew found the pandemic lockdown was the perfect time to renovate the garden that had become overgrown during his time away. The gravel design approach ended up being the ideal solution to reduce maintenance and allow him to grow more arid plants. “It’s a fun place to play around with a whole new palette of plants I haven’t grown before,” he says. ‘Skyracer’ purple moor grass (*Molinia caerulea* ssp. *arundinacea* ‘Skyracer’) adds height and whimsy to the garden with its 6- to 8-inch airy flower stalks that take on a gold color in autumn.

in the gravel for their roots to touch the soil below. He faithfully hand-watered the new plants to help them get established in the first year. This necessary task became a welcomed pandemic activity while working remotely. Two years later, the plants were thriving in the hostile environment. Yet, weeds were virtually nonexistent except for a few stragglers along the edges of the path and lawn.

Still, Andrew shares that the first year was plenty of trial and error as he experimented with a lot of single plants. One of the biggest challenges was the deer pressure. He says they had been bold enough to eat the pansies in the window boxes along the front of the house, so they also devoured new gravel garden plants including great burnet, hens and chicks, and ice plants.

"It became a survival of the fittest," he says. In year two, he repeated and massed more of the survivors to create cohesive design throughout the garden. He added additional deer-proof allium, little bluestem, lavender, spurge, ironweed, and wild quinine—all fragrant with highly textural foliage which deer don't like.

With the design, Andrew found he preferred wide versus tighter plant spacing throughout the gravel.

"I have lots of voids and spaces for a more modern aesthetic," he says. "I like the negative spaces the gravel creates."

Surprisingly, not all understood Andrew's "radical" garden project. A *New York Times* story on his and Jeff Epping's gardens generated 300 online comments, from skeptics and more curious types.

Undeterred, Andrew welcomed the questions and opportunity to share the lessons he learned in forging his gravel gardening approach. In talks, garden tours, and articles, he now shares tips for success and champions gravel gardens' aesthetic and environmental attributes.

He continues to visit more gravel gardens, examining them with a new lens and bringing home ideas to refine his own garden. The latest inspirations were to add spring bulbs and pockets of sandy soil for a few self-sowing sea hollies and California poppies.

"I'm in no rush to finish and am perfectly happy to dabble, tweak, and edit this garden over the next ten years," he says. "I enjoy the process."

ABOVE Andrew designed artistic plantings using deer-proof, xeric plants in a desert-esque environment. "It became a survival of the fittest," he says. **OPPOSITE** For twenty-five years, Andrew Bunting, vice president of horticulture at Pennsylvania Horticultural Society, has tried multiple garden styles at his ⅓-acre property called "Belvidere." As he traveled for work, gravel gardens kept popping up on his radar, so he decided to try one at home.

The Essential Gravel Layer

HOW IT WORKS: The gravel layer functions much like a sandy beach. Consider how a beach is hot on the surface—often too hot to walk on. Yet, when you dig your toes in a few inches, the sand feels cool and moist. These same dynamics happen in the gravel garden where drought-tolerant plants thrive in the heat reflected from the gravel yet tap into the cool moisture in the soil below the gravel. Plants adapt to these extreme conditions by sending roots deep into the soil to access water. The gravel also acts as a weed barrier by not exposing soil to weed seeds to germinate. The layer's lack of nutrients also results in plants growing more modestly and not flopping or needing to be staked as in more lush settings. This slower, more deliberate growth means plants often thrive longer and become more resilient to pests and diseases.

GRAVEL TYPES: Gravel rock is stone that has been mined from a quarry and crushed into varying-size pieces. These remnants are sifted, then sorted by size ranging from pea size (⅜-inch) to several inches. The colors vary depending on the stone. For example, limestone is usually a light buff color, while granite is darker gray. Water also changes gravel's coloring, whether deeper when wet or chalkier when dry. Gravel shapes range from round to irregular. To visually tie the garden to its setting, choose gravel from regional quarries. Local gravel will also have a lower carbon footprint than gravel shipped from across the country. When available, granite gravel is the preferred choice for its durability and range of gray tones. Limestone gravel is a secondary option, since it is softer and more likely to crush under constant pressure. River rock and pea gravel are naturally rounded stones. They perform similarly in a gravel garden, but be aware their rounded shape can cause them to move and hence be less stable for walkways.

GRAVEL SIZES: Select ¼- to ⅜-inch chip gravel (no fines) for gravel gardens. If the gravel is too small, then the gravel layer will hold moisture. If the gravel is too large, then pore spaces can accumulate organic matter where weed seeds can germinate. Gravel pieces should all be the same size, so the pieces remain loose and allow water to move through. Think of it as marbles in a jar.

GRAVEL DEPTH: The depth is key in gravel gardens. A mere mulching will not work. If too shallow, the roots of weed seedlings will reach the soil below. If the gravel is too deep, the plants struggle. The ideal depth—4 to 5 inches—discourages weeds from finding a foothold while minimizing stormwater runoff and directing available water to where roots can use it.

OTHER NOTES: Avoid using any landscape fabric beneath the gravel. The fabric will prevent plants from rooting in, as well as keep the garden from absorbing stormwater runoff. Not to mention, there is nothing worse than seeing the edges of the black material poke through the stones.

BOTTOMLINE: Choose a gravel from a hard, regional stone that is ¼- to ⅜-inch in size.

ABOVE Two inches of locally sourced 3/8-inch washed gray granite gravel was tilled into the existing soil to improve drainage, then another 4 inches placed over that prior to planting.

TOP Before the renovation, invasive weeds had taken over Andrew's cottage-style meadow in his front yard. He removed the top 6 inches of topsoil, and the rhizomes and seeds went with it. BOTTOM Since this area of the gravel garden that borders the small lawn is not edged with a hard divider, it will require more maintenance as turfgrasses send roots and rhizomes into the open gravel layer.

1 Donkey tail spurge (*Euphorbia myrsinites*) is one of the hardiest and most drought-tolerant of spurge species. It's grown for its architectural form and shimmering silver foliage. Its milky white sap can cause dermatitis, so wear gloves when handling it. **2 Phenomenal® lavender** PHENOMENAL lavender (*Lavandula* × *intermedia* 'Niko', PHENOMENAL) is an excellent hardy and disease-resistant cultivar that is highly attractive to bees and butterflies but not deer. **3 Twistleaf yucca** (*Yucca rupicola*) is only native to a small area of Texas where it grows on dry limestone hillsides. Andrew's well-drained gravel garden provides the perfect conditions for it to thrive in the Philadelphia area. **4 Wild quinine** (*Parthenium integrifolium*) is a widespread U.S.-native species that is as tough as it is beautiful and attracts a plethora of bees, wasps, flies, beetles, and plant bugs. Its sandpapery, bitter-tasting leaves are ignored by deer and other mammals. **5 'Isla Gold' tansy** (*Tanacetum vulgare* 'Isla Gold') brightens up the garden with its brilliant golden foliage all season and button-like, yellow flowers aglow in summer. **6 Slender mountain mint** (*Pycnanthemum tenuifolium*) is native to eastern North America and grows in full sun in just about any soil. It is one of the best pollinator plants for gravel gardens. **7 Eastern prickly pear** (*Opuntia humifusa*) is native to the eastern and central United States and is extremely hardy and drought-tolerant. Gorgeous gold flowers in summer produce edible fruits in fall. **8 Pearly everlasting** (*Anaphalis margaritacea*) and 'Millenium' ornamental onion (*Allium* 'Millenium') offer attractive contrasting foliage throughout the season, and their showy flowers are a bonus in summer. **9 Plains prickly pear** (*Opuntia polyacantha*), native to the western United States and Canada, adds interesting architectural foliage and spines all year and large gorgeous yellow flowers in late spring.

RIGHT BLACKBIRD spurge (*Euphorbia* 'Nothowlee', BLACKBIRD) is an evergreen perennial with dark purple, velvety foliage that produces brilliant yellow-green rounded flower heads in spring.

LEFT 'J.C. Raulston' Parry's agave (*Agave parryi* 'J.C. Raulston') is a rare cultivar that Andrew is trialing in hopes the drier conditions of the gravel garden will help it thrive despite his wet winters.

OPPOSITE: TOP LEFT Chanticleer horticulturist Dan Benarcik, a longtime friend of Andrew's, designed and skillfully fabricated a unique iron and wood bench for his patio garden. TOP RIGHT Andrew inherited this interesting, tawny-colored, stone path that leads from the driveway to the front door. He planted an assortment of cascading perennials that visually soften the hard edges. BOTTOM LEFT The rich bluestone walk to the main entryway is a bit more formal with even path edges and cut joints. The random sizes and angled joints give the path just the right amount of informality to match the architecture of the cottage-style home and gravel garden. BOTTOM RIGHT A pair of carved sandstone spheres have aged well and support moss and lichens that grow as the weather dictates. Silvery donkey tail spurge contrasts beautifully with the stone and gravel.

RIGHT The centrally located patio makes a great place to sit and enjoy the garden or wait for guests to arrive. BELOW A huge blue star (*Amsonia hubrichtii*) and an Asian spicebush (*Lindera glauca* var. *salicifolia*) near the house were retained from the previous garden, both prized for their exceptional long-lasting, gold fall color.

SEAN CONWAY
Tiverton, Rhode Island

Renovated Retreat

Sean Conway's Rhode Island kitchen garden was once a television star, brimming with vegetables and overflowing with charm. Viewers of his gardening series, *Cultivating Life*, were captivated by the bean vines climbing an 8-foot tower, tomato plants rambling over A-frame trellises, and cut flowers creating vibrant pockets. But for Sean, the constant maintenance grew to be a burden.

"It was very productive, but being the center of the garden, it was a real challenge to keep it looking good all the time," he says. He started exploring ways to rework his labor-intensive garden once he moved on from the show.

In 2019, inspiration struck on a fortuitous walk through Chanticleer Garden in Pennsylvania. The "spectacular" gravel garden, with its beauty, texture, and drought-tolerant Mediterranean plants, was a revelation.

"It was a light bulb moment for me," says Sean.

Back home, he decided to experiment with the technique in a patch of gravel along a path in his vegetable garden. "I'm going to test these out and see how it goes without spending a ton of money," says Sean.

Right in the path's gravel, he planted a few plants including lavender, gaura, and betony. He observed how these drought-lovers thrived in the summer heat, a stark contrast to their struggles in the wet winters of his perennial borders. The success in the gravel was undeniable.

In 2020, during the pandemic, Sean embarked on a full-scale transformation. He cleared the existing 46-by-85-foot space, incorporated gravel into the top foot of soil, and graded the space with a central crown and sloping edges. Cobblestones framed the perimeter, and another foot of ¾-inch pea gravel, sourced locally, was spread in a top layer.

"The pea gravel is a native stone with multi colors," says Sean, noting that the stones' softer colors don't reflect the sun as harshly as some gravels.

Gone was the kitchen garden's ornate French fountain. Instead, Sean crafted a simpler one from a concave fieldstone, drilling a hole in the bottom and attaching a bubbler to the existing pump below. This new feature, much to his delight, became a magnet for birds.

"It attracts more birds than any feeder," says Sean.

Next, he started sketching a design beginning with open paths. "I wanted to walk through the garden, not just around it," he says.

He assembled a list of plants leaning on advice from experienced gravel garden friends. For impact, he chose tall, dramatic plants like 'Skyracer' moor grass, prairie dock, mullein, big and little bluestem, and rattlesnake master. He rounded out the palette with lavender, salvia, Mexican feather grass, spurge, coneflowers, self-sowing poppies, ageratum, and butterfly milkweed. He designated smaller plants like tassel flowers, lambs' ears, and thyme to line paths for closer inspection.

"These are delicate plants that would get swallowed up elsewhere," says Sean.

In 2021, planting commenced. Sean laid out the plants, allowing lots of negative space for the gravel to show.

"I wanted to see the gravel and use it as a background to show off the plants' structure," says Sean.

OPPOSITE Sean Conway's gravel garden is a creative playground to experiment with new plants and artful combinations. "I wanted to see the gravel and use it as a background to show off the plants' structure," says Sean.

Andrew found he preferred wide versus tighter plant spacing throughout the gravel. “I have lots of voids and spaces for a more modern aesthetic,” he says. “I like the negative spaces the gravel creates.”

Once a beautiful, yet labor-intensive, kitchen garden for the set of Sean's TV gardening series *Cultivating Life*, the transformed space has now become a more naturalistic showcase requiring much less work.

He intentionally planted the gravel garden in the spring to take advantage of the cooler temperatures and minimize the stress on the new plants. His consistent hand-watering during the first year ensured their establishment.

Today, the garden is a stunning tapestry with swaths of grasses punctuated by striking architectural plants and woven together with loose clusters of colorful flowering plants like salvia, coneflower, and lavender.

"When they come into bloom, they knit the whole garden together," says Sean.

The landscape's existing bordering elements—an impressive hedge of purple beech trees, six signature cylindrical hornbeams, two greenhouses, and the summerhouse—frame the gravel garden, making it the centerpiece.

"The gravel garden is now the focal point of everything," he says.

Now in its third year, the garden continues to inspire and spur his love of plants. The near absence of weeds is a welcome surprise, only occasional volunteers from garden plants self-seeding in the gravel. Another delightful discovery was the arrival of painted and snapping turtles nesting in the gravel.

"Word got out that the gravel is easy digging," jokes Sean.

The ever-changing palette adds to the intrigue. California poppies self-sow, and toadflax make surprising appearances, adding pops of color before disappearing in the summer heat, only to return next spring.

"I'm constantly adding and taking away," says Sean. "The gravel garden has really reignited my passion for gardening."

ABOVE Wider-spaced plantings of little bluestem (*Schizachyrium scoparium*) soften the strong architectural lines of rattlesnake master (*Eryngium yuccifolium*) and allow for stunning views of the garden from the summer house. **OPPOSITE** Sean is intrigued by the garden's ever-changing palette. "I'm constantly adding and taking away," says Sean. "The gravel garden has really reignited my passion for gardening."

Garden Renovation: Breathe New Life into a Garden

Many gardeners yearn for a change. Perhaps you've tired of a high-maintenance garden, inherited a neglected garden, or lost a big shade tree. Maybe your children have outgrown their play area, or you simply desire a more eco-friendly space. A garden renovation can breathe new life into a garden, and a gravel garden can be the perfect solution. Here are a few tips for transforming your space.

ASSESS YOUR EXISTING SPACE. Before diving in, take stock of your current garden. Identify features you want to keep, like walkways, patios, fences, or water features. Are there overgrown shrubs or evergreens that need to go? Carefully consider the light conditions. Is there enough sunlight to support a gravel garden's typical drought-tolerant plants? Is there a water source nearby to water them during their first year? Look for existing drought-tolerant plants to save for the gravel garden.

DESIGN. Imagine how you'll use your renewed garden. Will it be a place for entertainment, relaxation, or simply enjoying a view from inside? How do you want to navigate it? Do you envision strolling through the space or creating a patio retreat? Consider both curb appeal and privacy when planning the layout. Sketch a design incorporating key elements like paths, water features, seating areas, and planting zones. Be realistic about your capabilities: will you handle the installation and initial care yourself or enlist the help of a designer or contractor?

DEFINING THE FOOTPRINT. Visualize the perimeter of your garden. How will you define its boundaries? A stone or brick edging, a driveway, walkway, sidewalk, or even your house foundation can all serve this purpose and hold the gravel layer in place. Decide whether you'll work within the existing footprint or expand or reduce the size.

PLANTING STRATEGIES. While you prepare the space, temporarily relocate the plants you plan to keep. Repot them in containers or dig a temporary trench. Source new plants from local or online nurseries. Ideally, purchase all plants at once for a one-day installation, minimizing stress on the plants. Schedule thorough watering for the new additions, continuing as necessary (often daily) until they're established. A temporary irrigation system can be a helpful tool.

FINISHING TOUCHES. Personalize your garden with details like a bench, sculpture, and informative signage to enhance its beauty and show cues for care. Have fun tweaking the garden as it matures. Edit overzealous self-sowers and replace struggling plants to maintain a thriving oasis.

ABOVE Today, the garden is a stunning tapestry with swaths of grasses punctuated by striking architectural plants and woven together with loose clusters of colorful flowering plants like salvia, coneflower, and lavender. "When they come into bloom, they knit the whole garden together," says Sean.

When Sean adds new plants, he creates a reverse volcano in the hole with a mixture of soil and pea gravel and plants into it. Once the plants have established a bit, he spreads the surrounding gravel back around the plant.

❶ **'Linda' anise hyssop** (*Agastache* 'Linda'), one of Sean's favorites, is a hybrid between *A. rupestris* and *A. rugosa* and sports scads of magenta-to-purple flowers on 30-inch stalks. He has found it to be very reliable in his climate, which hasn't been true for other anise hyssop cultivars. ❷ **Golden oats** (*Stipa gigantea*), a gorgeous ornamental grass, is often seen in English gardens where it is coveted for its elegant flower stalks that gracefully move in the slightest of breezes. It is rarely seen in the United States but is growing beautifully in Sean's gravel garden. ❸ **Manor House ornamental oregano** (*Origanum laevigatum* 'Herrenhausen') has a delightful sprawling habit with rich, rose-colored flowers. Planted near walkways, its foliage emits a pleasing herbal fragrance when lightly brushed against. ❹ **Royal catchfly** (*Silene regia*) is a U.S. native with brilliant red flowers that hummingbirds can't resist. It requires excellent drainage to grow, so is quite happy growing in gravel in full sun or part shade. ❺ **'Green Jewel' purple coneflower** (*Echinacea purpurea* 'Green Jewel') produces elegant greenish-white flowers, which are especially rich in morning and evening light. ❻ **Tassel flower** (*Emilia coccinea*) is a self-seeding annual in the gravel garden and sprouts in late spring along path edges, where it doesn't get overshadowed and shaded out by more vigorously growing perennials. ❼ **American basketflower** (*Plectocephalus americanus*; formerly *Centaurea americana*) is a tall, showy U.S. native annual that reseeds in the gravel. Horticulture professor Jared Barnes, a resident of Texas where it blooms by the thousands, may describe its flowers best: "The lavender flowers are dazzling and pompous in appearance, like having an exploded firework frozen in time." ❽ **'Tanna' greater burnet** (*Sanguisorba officinalis* 'Tanna') produces hundreds of small button-like burgundy flowers atop 2- to 3-foot whimsical, wispy stems. It is especially nice intermingled with ornamental grasses. ❾ **'Cream' California poppy** (*Eschscholzia californica* 'Cream') a warm, white-flowered form of the orange-flowered western U.S. native, is right at home in Sean's dry gravel. Plants survive only mild winters, but they readily self-sow each spring.

For impact, Sean chose tall, dramatic plants like 'Skyracer' moor grass, golden oat grass, prairie dock, mullein, bluestem grasses, and rattlesnake master. He rounded out the palette with lavender, meadow sage, Mexican feather grass, spurge, coneflowers, self-sowing poppies, ageratum, and butterfly milkweed. He designated smaller plants like tassel flowers, lambs' ears, and thyme to line paths for closer inspection. The towering 10-foot-tall airy flowers of prairie dock (*Silphium terebinthinaceum*) (bottom) are solidly anchored in the gravel by deep taproots beneath its bold, textured, dark green rosette of foliage.

Sean enhances the naturalistic design with several cues for care, including gravel paths, stone edging, six impressive cylindrically pruned hornbeams and a precisely clipped hedge of purple beech.

To create the garden, the existing 46-by-85-foot space was cleared. Gravel was incorporated into the top foot of soil and graded with a central crown and sloping edges. Cobblestones frame the perimeter, and another foot of 3/8-inch pea gravel, sourced locally, was spread in a top layer. "The gravel garden is now the focal point of everything," says Sean.

ONE WAY

Gravel in the City

SWARTHMORE COLLEGE
Swarthmore, Pennsylvania

New Spin for a Roundabout

As drivers zip around the roundabout at Swarthmore College, many slow down to admire its striking prairie plantings and offer praise for what they consider "the most beautiful roundabout ever." This gravel garden, a centerpiece of Swarthmore's updated traffic design, was installed in 2017 as a part of a project to accommodate a new inn and improve traffic flow.

"The roundabout presented a bit of a landscape design challenge," says Adam Glas, Swarthmore's garden supervisor. "We wanted it to look beautiful, but we also needed it to be as low-maintenance as possible."

Swarthmore's grounds and horticulture team, responsible for the college's 425-acre campus—including 125 acres of active gardens and the Scott Arboretum—was tasked with the new design. Given their extensive responsibilities, they sought low-maintenance options to minimize additional work.

Initially, the team planted trees and shrubs such as eastern red cedars and Kentucky coffee trees to meet the Pennsylvania Department of Transportation's requirements. However, they thought the trees and evergreens alone lacked the visual "punch" for such a prominent campus location.

Jeff Jabco, Swarthmore's grounds director and horticulture coordinator, proposed trying "gravel culture," a technique he learned from Cassian Schmidt at Hermannshof in Weinheim, Germany. He was intrigued by Cassian's research work focusing on growing hardy, drought-tolerant perennials in a gravel substrate. He even invited Cassian to lecture for the arboretum about his low-maintenance gravel gardening approach. The concept seemed ideal for this space.

To implement the design, the team removed 6 inches of soil from the roundabout, added 2 inches of locally sourced ½-inch tumble gravel, then tilled it into the subsoil. Next, they leveled the gravel soil mix and topped it with a 4-inch layer of gravel. They selected a plant palette based on Cassian's formula, prioritizing native prairie species. The palette was 5 percent structural plants like switch grass, little bluestem, bluestar, and false indigo; 35 percent companion plants such as salvia, blazing star, and asters; 50 percent ground-cover plants like perennial geranium and purple love grass; and 10 percent filler plants including threadleaf coreopsis and purple prairie clover.

Plants were spaced densely to ensure ground coverage following Cassian's recommended spacing of six to seven plants per square yard. They laid out the plants in a random fashion versus a grid to create a more natural look. "Cassian's philosophy was to really cover the ground, so you keep moisture in and shade out any weeds," explains Adam.

Although the team was initially uncertain about the success of some plants, especially since it was an unfamiliar technique, they adapted by replacing underperformers like Appalachian mountain mint and purple love grass with suitable alternatives. "We definitely had some failures initially, but that opened up opportunities to diversify and try other things," he says.

Several challenges emerged during the project. Sourcing appropriately sized plants—ideally quart-size—was crucial. Larger "babied" plants from nurseries tended to struggle in the harsh environment, while smaller landscape plugs

OPPOSITE This gravel garden, a centerpiece of Swarthmore College's updated traffic design, was installed in 2017 as a part of a project to accommodate a new inn and improve traffic flow.

As drivers zip around the roundabout, many slow down to admire its striking prairie plantings and offer praise for what they consider "the most beautiful roundabout ever." In May, just in time for graduation, the ornamental onions, meadow sage, and geraniums add a show-stopping wave of purple.

ONE WAY

lacked sufficient root mass. Additionally, work was restricted by state rules to weekdays between 9 a.m. and 3 p.m., necessitating a highly organized approach to the installation. Watering was another hurdle, as the team relied on a manual electric water tank due to the absence of an accessible water source. The team of gardeners doing the installation was careful to remove as much soil from the nursery-grown plants as possible to help prevent the introduction of weed seeds. This made it very important to keep these almost-bare-root plants watered for the first several weeks until establishment.

Another obstacle was managing some self-seeding plants in the chosen substrate. Asters, in particular, crowded out other species. "We found they seeded in very heavily, especially among the crowns of other plants," he said. "They were outgrowing and shading out a lot of other plants, so we ended up pulling all but 10 percent of them."

Over the past seven years, the gravel garden turned out to be a low-maintenance success. This past spring, the team contracted out for a gravel refresh due to organic-matter buildup and subsequent weed pressure, reducing the need for weeding from monthly to only a couple times a year.

The effectiveness of the roundabout gravel garden has inspired the team to create more gravel gardens across campus, including parking lot mediums and areas along sidewalks where grass grew poorly.

"The gravel gardens really speak to the arboretum's mission to grow the best plants in the mid-Atlantic region and inspire people with different gardening techniques to take home," says Adam.

ABOVE Tough, drought-tolerant perennials like Deam's black-eyed Susan, millenium ornamental onion, and Hubricht's bluestar were closely planted together to form this beautiful and resilient tapestry. OPPOSITE "The roundabout presented a bit of a landscape design challenge," says Adam Glas, Swarthmore's garden supervisor. "We wanted it to look beautiful, but we also needed it to be as low-maintenance as possible."

ONE WAY

Medians and sidewalks: The design uses wide swaths of larger-statured perennials like Decadence® 'Lemon Meringue' false indigo (*Baptisia* Decadence® 'Lemon Meringue') and blue star (*Amsonia hubrichtii*) to take up more space and reduce maintenance while adding beauty to the landscape designs. **OPPOSITE** The success of the roundabout gravel garden has inspired the team to create more gravel gardens across campus, including parking lot mediums and areas along sidewalks where grass grew poorly.

Gravel Gardening FAQ

Does it help to fertilize plants? Most plants perform better without fertilizers, which cause them to grow too tall and flop.

How deep should plants be planted in the gravel? Insert the plants so their crowns are even or just below the surface of the gravel layer.

How far apart should plants be placed? Plants should be spaced anywhere from 12 to 16 inches on center, depending upon their mature sizes. Tighter-than-usual spacing is best. Very large-growing species like amsonia and baptisia can be spaced farther apart.

When do you do the annual cutback? Wait until late winter or early spring to cut back dried plants. Haul out the material and place it in an area where overwintering insects can emerge before adding it to an active compost pile. If you are tight on space, create small piles within your regular garden beds—after insects emerge, the decomposing organic matter can become part of the mulch layer.

Do you use landscape fabric? No landscape fabric is used in this gravel garden technique. Plants need to root deeply into the soil under the 4- to 5-inch gravel layer that acts as a barrier to weed seed germination.

Can a gravel garden work in shade? Gravel gardens work best in full sun where sun-loving drought-tolerant plants thrive. Trees tend to drop a lot of debris (bud scales, flower petals, fruit, etc.) during the growing season, which allows organic matter to build up in the gravel layer, resulting in an ineffective weed barrier.

Is maintaining a gravel garden really less work than a conventional planting? Beyond the installation and early establishment of plants, the gravel garden's only maintenance task is the annual cutback in late winter or early spring. Otherwise, they need minimal weeding and water only during extreme droughts. This is much less work than annual mulching, edging, and weeding of conventional garden beds.

Do I have to remove 6 inches of soil from the entire garden? It is not necessary to remove the soil; just create a 6-inch tall border or edge to contain the 4- to 5-inch gravel layer.

What is the best-size plant to use in the gravel garden? The ideal pot size is 3½ to 4½ inches, quart-size, or a deep plug. These sizes typically hold plants with 4- to 5-inch root balls that ideally match the depth of the gravel layer. Larger potted plants can be used, but the root balls will have to be reduced to a 4- to 5-inch depth. This can be more difficult, time-consuming, and definitely more costly. Smaller pots or plugs can also be used, but they take longer to root into the soil, making them more vulnerable to drought stress as they get established.

I inherited a garden that has large (2 to 3 inches in diameter) stone mulch over landscape fabric around shrubs and perennials. Can I convert it to a gravel garden? Only if you remove the fabric and replace the stone with a smaller-diameter gravel. The space between individual pieces of larger gravel are so large that they allow debris to enter. This is hard to remove; organic matter builds up over time, resulting in weed seed germination and invasion.

Can a gravel garden be used as a rain garden? No, since the runoff water that is captured by a rain garden often carries soil sediment and other debris that would quickly fill the air spaces in the gravel layer, rendering it ineffective against weed seed germination and invasion.

It seems like some of the featured gravel gardens use different gravel compositions—is one better than another? Gravel types vary by region, and it's more sustainable to source gravel from a local quarry. Just make sure it is (1) ¼ to ⅜ inches in diameter, (2) a hard gravel that won't break down over time, and (3) washed of finer gravel particles so that consistent air space is maintained between gravel particles. Imagine a jar filled with marbles—no matter how much you shake it, you can't eliminate the air spaces between the individual marbles.

Can I plant annuals in my gravel garden to add more color throughout the growing season? Yes, try adding pockets of sandy soil to the gravel to plant annual seeds. Be aware these areas will also be vulnerable to weeds in future years. You could also try embedding a hollow cylinder, like a short (6- to 8-inch) clay or metal pipe, through the gravel layer and filling it with soil, then plant annual plugs or direct-sow annual seeds.

How long will a gravel garden last? Gravel gardens will last for years if they are maintained properly. If annual cleanups are not thorough and organic matter is allowed to build up, then the gravel layer may need to be replaced. However, Jeff has gravel gardens he installed more than fifteen years ago with no appreciable loss of weed suppression. Extend the life of the gravel layer by annually clearing away all dried plant material in late winter or early spring.

Does the gravel garden approach work in different climates? Gardeners are having success with gravel gardens in warm southern climates, hot desert climates, and cooler humid climates. The key is siting the garden in the right place (full sun with well-drained soils) and selecting regionally appropriate plants. Hotter climates may require more attention to watering new plants until they become fully established and scheduling installations during cooler months.

Doesn't the gravel make the garden hotter and less hospitable for the plants? No, the gravel actually helps keep the garden cooler. It shades the soil, and the air spaces between the gravel particles act as insulation, keeping the soil temperature lower. Later in the peak season, the plants shade the gravel, in turn cooling the soil beneath. Additionally, unlike organic mulches that can absorb a great deal of moisture, nearly all the rainwater reaches the soil, even during light showers.

How do you know how much to water new plantings? Water thoroughly three to five times a week for the first two to three weeks, possibly less if rainfall is abundant. Slowly wean the plants off irrigation over the following months as their roots grow deeper and wider into the soil beneath the gravel layer. During hot, sunny, or windy days, plants may wilt during the heat of the day, even if their root systems are saturated. Check the plants in the morning and if they are wilting, give them some water; if not, they should be fine for another day. If pressed for time, try setting up a simple temporary irrigation system with sprinklers and soaker hoses.

What is bare-rooting, and how does it relate to gravel gardens? To bare-root plants, gently remove all the soil before planting. This technique can help small plants quickly acclimate to a new environment. The key is to keep them well watered until they are established. A more modest approach is to peel off the top ½ to 1 inch of soil mix to rid yourself of dormant weed seeds that will be sure to germinate later. Also break apart bound root systems to encourage new roots to grow downward into the soil and not continue circling as they were in the pot. Put excess potting soil in a bucket—never mix it into the gravel.

ABOVE Plants were spaced at six to seven per square yard to ensure ground coverage. Planting this densely shades the gravel, which lessens weed seed germination, cools the gravel and soil beneath, and reduces evaporation by the sun hitting the exposed gravel surface. LEFT Standing here with Adam, Jeff Jabco--Swarthmore's grounds director and horticulture coordinator--proposed trying "gravel culture," a technique he learned from Cassian Schmidt at Hermannshof in Weinheim, Germany. Given his team cares for 125 acres on the campus, this low-maintenance option was appealing to minimize additional work.

Roadside Warriors

❶ **'Happy Days' sunflower** (*Helianthus* 'Happy Days') is a perennial sunflower with bright, cheery, double yellow and gold flowers. ❷ **Appalachian mountain mint** (*Pycnanthemum flexuosum*) is a beautiful native that is highly attractive to pollinators but not deer, who don't like its minty-scented foliage. ❸ **'Zagreb' threadleaf coreopsis** (*Coreopsis verticillata* 'Zagreb') can be an aggressive spreader over time. If planted in a parking lot island with competition from other strong growing perennials, it can be a great addition. ❹ **Purple love grass** (*Eragrostis spectabilis*) is a super drought-tolerant U.S. native admired for its hazy pinkish seed heads in late summer and fall. ❺ **Wild petunia** (*Ruellia humilis*) is nothing like the annual petunias in garden centers. This native prairie and open woodland species comes back year after year with long-lasting lavender petunia–like flowers. It can seed abundantly in mineral-rich gravel gardens. ❻ **'BLUE HEAVEN' little bluestem** (*Schizachyrium scoparium* 'MinnBlueA', BLUE HEAVEN) is an upright cultivar with cool, blue-green foliage which turns from red in summer and burgundy in fall. ❼ The whimsical spherical flowers of **'Purple Sensation' ornamental onion** (*Allium* 'Purple Sensation') orbit above other early spring bloomers. ❽ **'Hummelo' betony** (*Stachys officinalis* 'Hummelo') puts forth showy rose-lavender flowers in the summer atop clean, dark green basal foliage. After the flowers fade, the upright flower stalks remain to give interest to the fall and winter garden. ❾ **Red hot poker** (*Kniphofia*) is a South African native that has upright, hot-colored flowers that look like fire on a stick. All require good drainage, and many cultivars are adapted to various areas of the country. Richard Hawke of the Chicago Botanic Garden recently evaluated a multitude of cultivars and found several well-suited to the upper Midwest. His results can be found through the Garden's website: www.chicagobotanic.org.

LEFT AND BELOW The flowers of Deam's black-eyed Susan (*Rudbeckia fulgida* var. *deamii*) and an adult milkweed bug on the pods of butterfly milkweed (*Asclepias tuberosa*).

RIGHT The Swarthmore team adopted Cassian Schmidt's planting formula: 5 percent structural plants like switch grass and little bluestem; 35 percent companion plants such as meadow sage and blazing star; 50 percent ground-cover plants like perennial geranium and wild petunia, and 10 percent filler plants including threadleaf coreopsis and purple prairie clover.

NORTH
320
13'-9"
400
FEET

LEFT Despite being surrounded by asphalt and concrete, drought-tolerant prairie plants thrive in this harsh urban environment. **BELOW** An excellent choice for gravel gardens, rough blazing star (*Liatrus aspera*) thrives in the same dry, nutrient-poor soils it inhabits in the wild.

OPPOSITE Trees and shrubs add height, dimension, and year-round structure to the design. They also occupy space for this big area, which helps reduce maintenance. Woody plants cost less per square foot to maintain than herbaceous perennials. 'Grey Owl' red cedar (*Juniperus virginiana* 'Grey Owl'), prized for its beautiful, blue-green evergreen foliage, is an excellent shrubby conifer for difficult sites. It is extremely heat- and drought-tolerant, as well as being tolerant of salt spray, salt-laden snowmelt, and runoff--important attributes in urban plantings near roadways and parking lots where de-icing salts are heavily used.

“The gravel gardens really speak to the arboretum’s mission to grow the best plants in the mid-Atlantic region and inspire people with different gardening techniques to take home,” says Adam. ‘Purple Sensation’ ornamental onion (*Allium* ‘Purple Sensation’) and its purple lollipop flowers hover above the dark pink flowers of ‘Karmina’ geranium (*Geranium* x *cantabrigiense* ‘Karmina’) and other herbaceous plantings that are yet to bloom in spring.

Rutgers Ave

WATER UTILITY HEADQUARTERS and GOODMAN POOL
Madison, Wisconsin

The Power of Public Beautification

In Wisconsin's state capital, gravel gardens are becoming a creative, maintenance-saving landscape technique for several public beautification projects. At the municipal waterworks building, a fountain was converted into a tiered gravel garden. And at the city's public pool, a series of parking lot islands were transformed into more gravel gardens. According to Megan McCrumb, lead ecologist for the City of Madison Parks Department, "gravel gardens can be a time investment up front, but a big maintenance savings long term."

Tiered Gravel Garden in Former Fountain

In 2005, Madison's Water Utility Department added a three-tiered water fountain and gurgling aquifer-inspired sculpture in front of its new municipal water building. It seemed like the perfect entry feature for this sustainable building built on pylons atop a former landfill.

"The fountain became a maintenance nightmare as the ground settled and an abundance of neighborhood cottonwood seeds and debris from the adjacent brush processing site blew in to regularly clog the pump," says Dan Rodefeld, the water utility's operations manager. "We got to a point where we were spending a lot on repairs and still kept losing water."

That's when he and maintenance supervisor Doug VanHorn decided to convert the 800-square-foot fountain into a garden. They called on Olbrich Botanical Gardens, a public-private partnership between the City of Madison Parks Division and the Olbrich Botanical Society, to discuss ideas. In 2021, they met with Jeff Epping, who was then Olbrich Gardens' horticulture director. He showed them several low-maintenance gravel gardens they'd created at the public garden and suggested they might be a good solution for the fountain. Doug and Dan were hooked.

"It was perfect," says Doug. "We can have this tiered, weedless flower garden and still keep the original art feature."

Jeff worked with them to develop a plan for the fountain's conversion to a multi-level gravel garden. "It was kind of like we had this giant planter," Doug recalls about the tiered, concrete space.

Fortunately, the water utility's maintenance team had all the necessary equipment, including a concrete hammer drill and backhoe, and all the project experience to prep the site. They just leaned on Jeff to select and source the plants.

With plants on order, the team cleared out the fountain and used the hammer drill to make multiple holes in the concrete base for plenty of drainage.

Next, they used the backhoe to add a base layer of soil in each tier, then topped off the tiers with 6 inches of chip gravel. The team picked up the plant order, and Jeff arranged the plants on-site and taught them about planting in the gravel. Dan's team then went to work digging the holes and placing the plants in the gravel. Rounded boulders were added as accents throughout. Once complete, a night crew member watered the gardens every three to four days until the plants were established.

OPPOSITE In Wisconsin's state capital, gravel gardens are becoming a creative, maintenance-saving landscape technique for several public beautification projects, including this renovated fountain-turned-gravel garden at the municipal waterworks building.

The City of Madison Waterworks' failing 800-square-foot fountain became a giant container for a new gravel garden. "It was perfect," says Doug. "We can have this tiered, weedless flower garden and still keep the original art feature."

Today, the tiered gardens are a great source of joy for the building's sixty-some employees and the many visitors that come to the building for meetings in the conference room overlooking the gardens.

"We don't deal with this kind of stuff every day, so we were a little skeptical," says Doug. "But it's worked out well—the garden is flourishing, and we have hardly any maintenance." They simply cut back the plants in early spring and pull a handful of weeds a couple times a year.

One tip from Doug: "It helps having a horticulture pro in your corner to advise on the project. Otherwise, it would have been tough to do this on our own."

Lower-Maintenance Approach for Pool's Parking Lots

When the new zero-entry Goodman Pool was completed in 2007, Madison's Parks Superintendent Eric Knepp enlisted the help of Olbrich Gardens to help finish the landscaped areas. The Olbrich team, led by Jeff, designed beautiful floral beds at the entrance, then proposed gravel gardens for the parking lot's weedy islands.

"The islands were an ideal place for gravel gardens, since they offered a low-maintenance approach, plus the islands were already filled with poor soil and enclosed by curbs," says Jeff. To prepare the islands, his team dug out several inches of soil around the edges. Next, they added a layer of gravel and began planting. The team carefully selected resilient plants and watered them thoroughly until they were established. The following year, the parks team took over maintenance under Jeff's direction.

Today, the islands require minimal upkeep. The team weeds in spring and cuts back plant material in fall.

"After a spring cleanup, they're pretty much hands-off for the rest of the growing season," says Anna Wilkie, arborist and landscaper who's been caring for the islands since 2018. This low-maintenance approach is a welcome benefit for the Parks Department, which oversees 136 beautification projects at the city's 291 parks.

The island gravel gardens have proven remarkably resilient in the parking lot environment. Native and drought-tolerant plants like purple prairie clover, calamint, prairie coreopsis, and Tennessee coneflowers thrive. Grasses such as little bluestem and prairie dropseed add texture, while amsonia, allium, Russian sage, and black-eyed Susan provide color. To maintain visibility, taller plants like cup plants and big bluestem were avoided. While common milkweed is a beloved native, its aggressive growth habit makes it unsuitable for the islands, and it is promptly removed when it occasionally seeds in from surrounding areas.

Compared with traditional mulched beds, Wilkie says gravel gardens offer several advantages. "Weeds are much easier to pull. And, since we're not using herbicides, we're creating a safer environment for pool visitors."

To prepare for winter, the parks team removes all plant debris to prevent organic-matter buildup in the gravel, reducing the potential of reseeding in the spring. They also coordinate with snowplow crews to keep snow piles away from the islands, minimizing unwanted salt and sand in the gravel.

The success of the Goodman Pool gravel garden islands demonstrates the potential for this low-maintenance landscaping approach for other municipal parking lots.

OPPOSITE Maintenance supervisor Doug VanHorn sits along the beautiful garden that he and his crew created. After many hours of costly repairs and potential demolition--the fate of many decorative water features in the United States--the fountain found new life as a gravel garden.

Raised Bed and Planter Gravel Gardens

Gravel gardens are an ideal option for raised islands in municipal or commercial parking lots and even large planters along office buildings. They both come with built-in borders to contain gravel, are already elevated for good drainage, and require low maintenance, yet offer an aesthetically pleasing landscape approach. Follow these tips for creating gravel gardens in these specialized situations.

PREP: First, remove all organic material from the surface of the soil, including weeds, especially tenacious perennial species with extensive root systems, like Canada thistle, Canada goldenrod, field bindweed, and quack grass. Second, grade the soil so the edges of the raised islands or planters are about an inch above the finished level of the gravel. This prevents the gravel from spilling out. Third, add ¼- to ⅜-inch washed gravel and spread evenly in a 4- to 6-inch layer.

PLANTING: Select tough, drought-tolerant plant species and space them about 15 to 18 inches apart throughout the gravel layer. If you prefer a sparser, more open look to the overall design, space plants farther from each other so they maintain open space after plants reach maturity. Quart-size potted plants work best. Before installing, remove the top inch of potting soil from the root mass, which in turn removes dormant weed seeds that will germinate later. Also, break apart tight circling roots and remove any loose soil from the garden, being certain not to mix it into the gravel. Dig holes in the gravel with gloved hands, then place the plants' roots in contact with the soil layer below. The crown of the plants should be even with the top of the gravel layer. Cover their root balls with gravel and thoroughly water them.

ESTABLISHMENT: Water is critical in establishing new plants in the gravel layer. Source water from a water wagon, a hose connected to a nearby faucet, or temporary access to a water hydrant. Make sure to thoroughly water three to five times a week during the first several weeks, then slowly wean the plants off irrigation in the following few months as their roots grow deeper and wider into the soil below the gravel layer. If pressed for time, try setting up a simple temporary irrigation system with sprinklers and soaker hoses.

MAINTENANCE: Spring is the most crucial time for maintaining your established gravel garden. As plants break dormancy and bulbs emerge, cut back all herbaceous plants to within 6 to 8 inches of the gravel, and remove the debris. Place the plant material in less-visible areas of your larger non-gravel gardens to preserve insect eggs and larvae, which will eventually decompose into mulch.

Use a battery-powered blower to clear organic matter from the gravel. This step is essential to prevent organic buildup, maintain air spaces, and preserve the gravel's weed-fighting properties.

Spring is also the best time to pull any weeds that have established in the crowns of desirable plants. Be careful not to mix soil into the gravel when removing weeds. Occasionally, seedlings may appear in the gravel; these are often the progeny of desirable plants and can be left to enhance the garden. For example, Carthusian pink (*Dianthus carthusianorum*) is a species that can add color and fill gaps when allowed to reseed.

SNOW REMOVAL: In northern regions during winter, instruct snow crews to plow snow away from the islands to prevent salt and sand from entering the gravel. Salt can damage plants, and sand can fill the gaps in the gravel, giving weed seeds what they need to germinate.

Olbrich Botanical Gardens' horticulture team coached the waterworks crew through the site-preparation process a few weeks prior to planting. On planting day, the horticulture team laid out all the plants and gave a planting demo to the crew, who then made quick work of it. "We don't deal with this kind of stuff every day, so we were a little skeptical," says Doug. "But it's worked out well--the garden is flourishing, and we have hardly any maintenance." Fun fact: The City of Madison has a long history in water innovation. In the 1880s, amid a cholera epidemic, Magnus Swenson developed a test to check the safety of backyard water wells. While citizens initially resisted the news of their bad water, they were eventually swayed, and a citywide waterworks was built, ensuring safe water for everyone.

❶ **Lead plant** (*Amorpha canescens*) is a shrubby native prairie species with attractive silvery foliage and blue flowers that are favored by a multitude of bees and other insects. Its seed heads are attractive throughout the fall and winter. ❷ **Little bluestem** (*Schizachyrium scoparium*) is among the most drought-tolerant of all our native prairie grasses, making it especially useful with the vagaries of climate change. It is also an important food source for grasshoppers and caterpillars of many native skipper butterfly species. ❸ **Purple prairie clover** (*Dalea purpurea*), another native prairie species, has beautiful rosy, pink flowers in midsummer and lasting seed heads that are attractive through fall. ❹ **New Jersey tea** (*Ceanothus americanus*) is another shrubby prairie species that has beautiful, fragrant pure white flowers in June that provide nectar to butterflies and hummingbirds. As the seed capsules dry, they mechanically eject their seeds up to several feet! ❺ Due to the very shallow soil profile of the fountain, a fine ¼-inch-grade-chip quartzite gravel was used to help reduce moisture loss but still repress weed seed germination. Six inches deep, the finer gravel has proven to be successful with plants flourishing without any supplemental watering. ❻ **Sea lavender** (*Limonium latifolium*) produces attractive airy sprays of lilac flowers in midsummer atop dark green rosettes of foliage, often remaining green through the winter. ❼ **'Herrenhausen' ornamental oregano** (*Origanum laevigatum* 'Herrenhausen') grows natively in dry, rocky mountainous regions in Turkey, so it is very tough and water-wise. Its aromatic, dark mauve flowers and dark green cascading foliage deters hungry deer and rabbits. ❽ **Russian sage** (*Perovskia atriplicifolia*) is a subshrub with silvery foliage that combines well with most perennials. It thrives in full sun and dry conditions. Few perennials bloom as long, and its showy blue flowers attract hummingbirds and numerous butterfly and bee species. ❾ **'Pica Bella' purple coneflower** (*Echinacea purpurea* 'Pica Bella') was ranked among the top-performing cultivars in coneflower evaluation trials at Mt. Cuba Center in Delaware. It is a compact grower and super floriferous, producing gorgeous orange-bronze coneflowers surrounded by deep pink ray flowers.

ABOVE Today, the tiered gardens are a great source of joy for the building's sixty-some employees and an excellent demonstration of water-wise gardening to the many visitors that come to the building for meetings in the conference room overlooking the gardens. **FAR LEFT** Deam's black-eyed Susans (*Rudbeckia fulgida* var. *deamii*) and 'Summer Beauty' ornamental onions (*Allium lusitanicum* 'Summer Beauty') commingle beautifully with fine-textured ornamental grasses offering diverse flower forms and soothing colors. **LEFT** Purple prairie clover (*Dalea purpurea*) and its flowers bring more life to the garden, sharing its pollen with a busy leafcutter bee.

ABOVE The islands were an ideal place for gravel gardens, since they offered a low-maintenance approach, plus the islands were already filled with poor soil and enclosed by curbs. To prepare the islands, they dug out several inches of soil around the edges to make room for the 5-inch gravel layer and then began planting.

OPPOSITE: TOP When the new Goodman Pool was completed in 2007, Madison's Parks enlisted the help of Olbrich Botanical Gardens to help finish the landscaped areas. The Olbrich team designed beautiful floral beds at the entrance, then proposed gravel gardens for the parking lot's weedy islands. **BOTTOM LEFT** The island gravel gardens have proven remarkably resilient in the parking lot environment. After the first two years, the islands have not been watered and have thrived despite two record-breaking droughts in recent years. In winter, it is important to not plow snow into the gardens, since over time the sand, salt, and other debris will fill the voids in the gravel and render them useless in preventing weed invasion; seedlings will easily germinate in the organic matter-laden gravel. **BOTTOM RIGHT** Today, the islands require minimal upkeep, with a light spring weeding and fall cutback. "After a spring cleanup, they're pretty much hands-off for the rest of the growing season," says Anna Wilkie, arborist and landscaper.

Native and drought-tolerant plants like purple prairie clover, black-eyed Susan, prairie coreopsis, and purple coneflowers thrive. Grasses such as little bluestem and prairie dropseed add texture, while amsonia, calamint, ornamental onion, and Russian sage provide color.

ADOPT A LOT PROGRAM
Chicago, Illinois

New Potential for Vacant Lots

When Annamaria Leon, co-owner of Homan Grown gardening social enterprise, talked with residents about their wishes for transforming vacant lots in Chicago's west- and south-side neighborhoods, she heard hopes for a green space to read, gather for picnics, and take meditative walks. Today, these dreams are becoming a reality.

"To me, a vacant lot is an opportunity—even a community asset—versus a blight," says Annamaria, project co-leader who together with business partner Pastor Reshorna Fitzpatrick and designer Chris Abraham introduced the city to the concept of gravel gardens as a low-maintenance approach to greening its growing number of vacant lots.

With more than 10,000 vacant lots, Chicago, like many cities, faced increasing health and safety risks associated with the abandoned spaces. Industry had moved out, many people followed, and buildings started to decline, eventually leaving behind vacant lot after vacant lot. The abandoned spaces increasingly became hangouts for drug trafficking, gang activity, and illegal dumping.

As city officials looked for solutions, they explored other cities' revitalization programs and learned greening efforts helped decrease violent crime by up to 40 percent and increased a sense of security by as much as 58 percent. Encouraged, they engaged crews from Greencorps Chicago, a city program focused on environmental stewardship and workforce training, to mow the vacant lots and build fences. While aiming for safety, the approach oftentimes backfired. The fences made residents feel excluded and became targets for vandalism. In addition, constant mowing became cost-prohibitive. This led Greencorps and other city officials to explore alternative solutions, including gravel gardens.

Annamaria invited city officials to tour the large-scale gravel gardens at Argonne National Laboratory, designed by landscape architect David Yocca and plantsman Roy Diblik. They then visited two successful Chicago greening projects—Kenwood Gardens (designed by Chris) and the Mamie Till-Mobley Forgiveness Garden. Both engaged the community and featured low-maintenance designs and tough plants. At Kenwood, they learned how artist Theaster Gates and his Rebuild Foundation purchased thirteen contiguous lots on the south side, then transformed them into a low-touch, naturalistic garden with spaces for concerts, yoga, and art. At the Forgiveness Garden, they visited newly installed parkway gravel gardens and learned how the low-maintenance concept was being expanded to green more parkways throughout the West Woodlawn neighborhood.

Inspired, the city embraced an Adopt A Lot program to revitalize city-owned vacant lots on blocks that have historically experienced the highest rates of violence. They contracted Annamaria and Reshorna to partner with community-based organizations and neighbors to establish these safe, green spaces.

"We wanted to create beautiful spaces on these vacant lots, yet many sites had no access to water and no one to steward them," says Annamaria. "The gravel gardens took the focus off maintenance and allowed the community groups to enjoy green spaces without a lot of care."

OPPOSITE Chicago's Adopt A Lot program embraces gravel gardens as a low-maintenance way to green the city's rising number of vacant lots. 'Butterfly Magnet' meadow blazing star (*Liatris ligulistylis* 'Butterfly Magnet') cascades over a gravel pathway.

Project leaders Pastor Reshorna Fitzpatrick (left) and Annamaria Leon (right) partnered with community groups and neighbors to create these safe, green spaces. “To me, a vacant lot is an opportunity--even a community asset--versus a blight,” says Annamaria.

Homan Grown brought together a project team to work with Greencorps crews, including garden designers Chris Abraham (72 Seasons) and Leo Boler, and horticulture advisers Roy Diblik, Jeff Epping, and Jens Jensen. To get started, they toured the lots designated by the city and sorted which ones were appropriate for gravel gardens. Annamaria and Reshorna met with residents and community groups to map out their wishes for how to use the lots.

"We challenged residents to let their imaginations go wild and turn these vacant lots into places where they could come and have conversations and experience a sense of peace here in these urban settings," says Reshorna.

Some envisioned simple pocket parks while others planned larger community spaces with picnic areas, performance spaces, food-truck parking, little libraries, and meditation paths. Chris and Leo designed a straightforward, adaptable plan featuring trees, pathways, and raised-bed gravel gardens.

"It's a simple design to allow the Greencorps crew discretion to create their own combinations," says Chris. "By the end of the summer, they were designing their own gardens, calling plants by their Latin names, and competing to bump up daily planting totals."

Within the gravel garden's base layer of prairie grasses, they created blocks and mixes of tough, flowering perennials including dianthus, allium, aster, monarda, goldenrod, coneflower, bee balm, and yarrow.

"We chose stunners and durable plants," says Chris, adding the goal was to achieve a succession of blooms from April to October.

Annamaria and Reshorna sourced the plants locally from Homan Grown's nursery, Intrinsic Perennials, Northwind Perennial Farm, Midwest Groundcovers, and other local nurseries. Greencorps prepped the sites by clearing invasive weeds, building timber frames, then spreading the gravel layer within the frames. On installation days, Chris and Leo worked with Greencorps crews to plant hundreds of perennials. They explained this new technique to the crew—creating a hole in the gravel, shaking off excess soil around the root ball, placing the plant roots in contact with the soil, then covering the plants with gravel.

The first garden was an instant showstopper even though the crew and neighbors questioned whether the small plants would thrive in the harsh gravel environment.

"Nothing's going to grow there, the neighbors would say," says Chris. Yet ever optimistic, he just smiled, knowing time would tell a different story.

The plants started to thrive within weeks, to the delight of the crew. They kept planting more gardens, growing more confident and eventually tweaking designs. The double lots typically included two gravel gardens with up to 1600 plants, a central path, and trees planted in the back of the lot. By the end of summer 2023, the team completed nine gravel gardens across thirty-five lots, including many double lots in Humboldt Park and Englewood neighborhoods.

"When you walk into these gardens, there is a peace of mind, a freedom to breath, and a sense of calm that comes to the human spirit," says Leo.

A key to the gardens' success has been adaptability. At one site, they had a partially demolished house foundation. While the city initially wanted to jackhammer and remove it—a time-consuming and costly task—the designers saw the foundation as an asset and seized the perfect opportunity to create a gravel garden within the walls.

On another lot, the site was used by neighbors to work on their cars. The designers again improvised, thoughtfully considered the needs of the neighborhood, and provided a much-needed workspace between two gravel gardens.

Chris recalls comments from one Greencorps member involved in creating the gardens: "My whole life, I wanted to give back to my neighborhood but didn't know how. I feel like I can do this. Everybody showed us love."

The community has responded with enthusiasm to the revitalized lots. Leo recalls one neighbor who watched the transformation for three days and even heckled, "Y'all planting in rocks?!", then upon completion delivered two stacks of homemade sandwiches to the crew and complimented them on the parklike setting.

"It was the perfect example of what beauty can inspire in others," says Leo.

OPPOSITE Garden designers Chris Abraham (left) and Leo Boler (right) worked with Greencorps Chicago to install nine gravel gardens in two neighborhoods that historically experienced the highest rates of violence. When neighbors challenged, "Nothing's going to grow there," the two, ever optimistic, just smiled, knowing time would tell a different story.

The Value of Urban Green Spaces

IMPROVE PHYSICAL AND MENTAL HEALTH. Green spaces offer a respite from the concrete and technology of urban environments. They allow residents to reconnect with the natural world and in turn reduce stress, lower blood pressure, and improve overall mood.

BUILD COMMUNITY. Green spaces affect residents' quality of life and facilitate a sense of community. They foster human connections by offering a place for people to gather, interact, and break down cultural barriers.

PROMOTE BIODIVERSITY. Green spaces support a range of birds, insects, and wildlife by offering food and shelter. They often provide a critical link for migrating birds and pollinators.

REDUCE URBAN HEAT. Trees and plants cool temperatures through shading and evaporative cooling. They can counteract urban heat island effects, thus reducing the energy costs of cooling buildings.

IMPROVE WATER QUALITY. Urban greenery helps infiltrate stormwater, reduces flooding, and minimizes toxins entering public waterways.

REDUCE AIR POLLUTION. Trees and plants help mitigate poor air quality. They sequester carbon, capture air pollutants, produce oxygen, and can improve the climate of a local area.

ENHANCE SOIL. Plant roots bind soil particles together, helping prevent erosion. As old roots die and new ones grow, they create small pores to channel in water and air, as well as add organic matter and nutrients to the soil. Similarly, the top portions of the plants also decay and return organic matter back to the soil each year.

ABOVE The garden installations provide practical, hands-on work experience for Greencorps crews.

OPPOSITE: TOP LEFT Purple prairie clover (*Dalea purpurea*) is not only drought-tolerant, it's also a legume that can fix its own nitrogen--an important feature when living in lean environments. TOP RIGHT The vast majority of wasps are good for the garden and friendly to us, like this blue-winged wasp on wild quinine (*Parthenium integrifolium*). BOTTOM LEFT Abundant gardens bring people together and build community pride. BOTTOM RIGHT The beauty of gardens and the wonderment of insects like this cabbage white butterfly on a blazing star flower help improve mental and physical health.

Survival of the Fittest

❶ **'Sunset Boulevard' sedum** (*Sedum* × 'Sunset Boulevard'), with its thick bold foliage and burgundy stems, thrives in the well-drained soils of the gravel garden. ❷ **Wild quinine** (*Parthenium integrifolium*) attracts soldier beetles that provide natural pest control and feed on the pollen of many flowers. ❸ **Meadow blazing star** (*Liatris ligulistylis*) is a nectar source for the common buckeye butterfly. ❹ **White goldenrod** (*Solidago* × 'Sugar Kisses') shrugs off drought and blooms from summer until fall. ❺ Washed, chipped quartzite gravel (¼- to ⅜-inch) is an excellent choice for gravel gardens in the Chicago area. Here it is spread in a 4- to 5-inch layer.

❻ **Moonshine yarrow** (*Achillea* × 'Moonshine') and other summer-blooming silver-foliaged yarrows are well-suited for gravel and often repeat-bloom late in the season. ❼ **East Friesland meadow sage** (*Salvia nemorosa* 'Ostfriesland') puts on a stunning floral display in June, rests for a bit, then sporadically flowers until late fall. ❽ **'Garden Ghost' white sage** (*Artemisia ludoviciana* 'Garden Ghost') is an aggressive grower in fertile soils, but less so in the dry soils of gravel gardens. ❾ **Carthusian pink** (*Dianthus carthusianorum*) is one of the few perennials that reseeds in the gravel garden but is easily removed if you don't want more of it.

'New Moon' ornamental onion (*Allium* x 'New Moon') features clean blue-green foliage and whimsical lollipop flowers. It offers long-lasting blooms and a myriad of pollinators like this brown-belted bumblebee.

OPPOSITE 'Honeycomb' blue grama flowers (*Bouteloua gracilis* 'Honeycomb') form a hazy cloud of golden flowers over loose blocks of tough, bolder-textured flowering perennials like 'New Moon' ornamental onion (*Allium* x 'New Moon') and Carthusian pink (*Dianthus carthusianorum*), creating an ethereal and calming mood in the garden. "We chose stunners among durable plants to create beautiful gardens," says Chris.

TOP LEFT Dense blazing star (*Liatris spicata*) is one of more than fifty species of blazing stars (*Liatris*) that are native to the United States and provide food for a plethora of bees, butterflies, and other pollinators. **ABOVE** Pale purple coneflowers (*Echinacea pallida*) dance with 'Honeycomb' blue grama (*Bouteloua gracilis* 'Honeycomb'). **LEFT** Many sites have no access to water, so the designers chose resilient plants that thrive in heat and drought yet offer a succession of blooms from April to October. A simple inexpensive metal edging is used to contain gravel here but may need reinforcing from time to time.

Why invest in neighborhood gardens? Studies show urban greening projects can help decrease violent crime by up to 40 percent and increase the sense of security by as much as 58 percent.

CASSIAN SCHMIDT
Weinheim, Germany

Early Lessons from Dry Landscapes

Expert plantsman, landscape architect, and professor Cassian Schmidt has been at the forefront of redefining naturalistic garden design with his habitat-based planting approach, particularly when it comes to dry landscapes and gravel gardens. His groundbreaking work at Hermannshof, a botanical and trial garden located on 6 acres in Germany's Rhine Valley, has inspired a generation of naturalistic designers, including influential icons like Beth Chatto, Piet Oudolf, and Roy Diblik.

Cassian's approach is rooted in his careful study of natural habitats and how to replicate them aesthetically in garden design. And, in this world of climate change, more and more designers are adapting his innovative, scientifically led planting style for its sustainability and reduced maintenance.

"Initially I didn't call them gravel gardens," he says. The term carried negative connotations in Germany, as many residents replaced their lawns with a stark, plant-free layer of gravel. Some regions even banned them.

Nevertheless, Cassian created his first trial gravel gardens in 2001 and called them "dry landscapes," expanding on Hermannshof's habitat-themed plantings. He re-created dry landscapes from his travels to the Alps, Pyrenees, Kyrgyz Steppe, and Mediterranean garigue scrublands, where he observed a "mineral layer" or gravel layer as a common theme. "In these rocky drylands," he explained, "you find this surface layer of course rocks that break down with frost and rain, gradually washing smaller pieces down to plants' roots."

To replicate these conditions, Cassian experimented using a 3-inch layer of granite and porphyry gravel (1⁄4- to 3⁄8-inch) from a local quarry to test a new maintenance approach in a steppe-inspired planting of salvia and achillea. Here, he changed from a conventional method of adding compost and providing regular irrigation to a more stress-based concept that mimics the natural conditions of a steppe landscape. The main factors were no irrigation, no fertilizer or compost, mineral mulching, removing the organic plant remains from the site in late winter, and no soil disturbance.

The results were surprising. The maintenance required for the gravel-layered planting was just 3.5 minutes per square meter, compared to seventeen minutes for the conventional planting. "By creating a stressful environment with no water and an infertile gravel layer, we significantly reduced maintenance," says Cassian. "This is the secret of any gravel garden."

Beyond saving time, Cassian discovered the gravel layer improved drainage and plant performance, particularly in winter. He initiated a second trial garden with the plantings in a lean substrate with 0 to 10 percent organic matter. "It doesn't make sense to install a gravel garden on a nutrient-rich, heavy loamy soil," says Cassian referencing Beth

OPPOSITE Expert plantsman, landscape architect, and professor Cassian Schmidt has been at the forefront of redefining naturalistic garden design with his habitat-based planting approach, particularly when it comes to dry landscapes and gravel gardens. Pictured here is his groundbreaking work at Hermannshof, a botanical and trial garden located on 6 acres in Germany's Rhine Valley.

“In nature, I personally love these dry, wide-open landscapes and see so much potential for these environments and their diverse plants in our stony inner cities,” says Cassian, who has introduced many drought-tolerant plant species into the garden industry, including various coneflower species. The North American Prairie Garden at Hermannshof shows a full complement of echinacea species.

Chatto's successful gravel garden built on a former parking lot with a free-draining gravelly substrate.

Looking forward, he envisioned several applications for gravel gardens in urban spaces where soils are being replaced during construction projects. "In median strips and roundabouts, it makes sense to bring in engineered soils with crushed gravel or recycled material," says Cassian. His experiments continued with different gravel sizes (0- to 1¼-inch), different substrate mixes with varying degrees of sand and compost, and different plants.

One notable finding was the impact of the gravel layer on plant diversity. After five years, a trial with a gravel mulch layer showed the least loss in plant composition, while the no-mulch trial saw a significant 40 to 50 percent loss. He attributes this to a few competitive plants reseeding and taking over the planting.

"Along with light, water, and soil, plant species competition levels play a key role in guiding plant communities," says Cassian, explaining that when plants in nature are free of competition, the best-adapted species are more likely to overtake less adaptable species. He conducted a five-year study of four mineral soil substrates with an organic content of 10, 20, and 30 percent volume and an additional variant of zero volume with a 3-inch gravel mulch layer. The results showed that the plots with only 10 percent and 0 percent had the best performance in terms of plant diversity. "That shows if you add more nutrients, you lose diversity," he said. "This is a paradox that lean, less-fertile soils have species richness and give us more reason to install these lean species diverse systems."

Cassian also observed that the coarseness of the gravel layer could be adjusted for different goals. A course layer suppresses weeds, while a finer, sand-like layer allows for reseeding. "The reseeding really depends on the coarseness of the surface layer," he emphasizes.

Moreover, plants grown with a gravel layer tended to grow larger than those without gravel. "The most logical reason is that microorganisms stay nice and cool under the mulch layer, where they thrive and process nutrients that are always available to the plants," says Cassian. The readily available nutrients led to consistent growth, with plants being 25 to 30 percent taller than those in the unmulched area.

Cassian also found that spacing plays a crucial role in the success of gravel gardens. He recommends wider spacing, suggesting six to eight perennials or two to three subshrubs per square meter. This mimics the natural distribution he observed of plants in dry, stressful environments, where coverage only reaches 50 percent.

Cassian's experiments even extended to using lightweight lava rock, ideal for rooftop applications. On Lanzarote in the Canary Islands, he found that vineyards covered in black lava rock were able to thrive without precipitation by using the porous rocks' air pockets to capture the moisture from the nighttime dew. Furthermore, he continues to observe others' experiments with different gravel layer materials, including a French project using upcycled asphalt and the Knepp Castle project using repurposed building materials as the mulch layer and substrate.

In recent years, Cassian and his wife, Bettina Jaugstetter, a landscape architect, have personally applied these gravel garden principles to urban projects in Germany, including large streetscapes in Bensheim and Mannheim, as well as an ecological campus at ABB's technology headquarters in Ladenburg. They are currently working on two new initiatives: a naturalistic woodland in Korea with integrated gravel gardens, and a former roadway in the German mining city of Mainz that's being transformed into a park featuring islands of plantings in crushed asphalt concrete with accents of larger asphalt and concrete chunks.

For the 2023 German garden show at Mannheim situated on the former American military site Spinelli Barracks, Bettina transformed several long, 32-foot-wide concrete driveways as a planting experiment. A 6.5-foot-wide median strip in the middle was cut out and transformed into three 1200-foot-long, linear gravel beds, planted with a mix of stress-tolerant steppe, dry prairie, and native plants, subdivided in three different color schemes (blue, yellow, and pink). Bettina reused the free-draining gravel layer under the concrete surface as substrate, adding only a top layer of 6 to 8 inches of porous mineral substrate without an additional gravel mulch layer.

Looking ahead, Cassian is especially optimistic about the role of gravel gardens in supporting pollinators, which are drawn to the gravel layer and mineral sandy substrate for burrowing and nesting. Gravel gardens' ability to support a diverse plant mix is another pollinator benefit. He recommends boosting plant diversity by combining native and non-native plants.

"With a 60 percent native and 40 percent non-native combination, you widen the flowering range for insects," says Cassian. He explains that especially in Europe, native plants were lost in the Ice Age, so we have to fill the flowering gaps with plants from similar habitats around the world.

For the future of gravel gardens, Cassian sees the greatest opportunities in rooftops, streetscapes, traffic circles, and other inner-city environments like former industrial sites, repurposed railways, and stormwater infiltration basins. He continues to champion this sustainable style for greening our cities as he designs public green spaces and shares his research at horticulture and design symposia internationally.

"In nature, I personally love these dry, wide-open landscapes and see so much potential for these environments and their diverse plants in our stony inner cities," Cassian concludes.

Cassian's approach is rooted in his careful study of natural habitats and how to replicate them aesthetically in garden design. He re-created dry landscapes from his travels to the Alps, the Kyrgyz Steppe (top), and rocky scrub in Turkey (bottom), where he observed a "mineral layer" or gravel layer as a common theme. **ABOVE RIGHT** Cassian Schmidt gives a tour of the innovative gardens that he designed at Hermannshof.

In recent years, Cassian and his wife, Bettina Jaugstetter, also a landscape architect and landscape designer, have applied gravel garden principles to urban projects in Germany, including large streetscapes in Bensheim and Mannheim, as well as an ecological campus at ABB's technology headquarters in Ladenburg (opposite).

For BUGA, the biennial German garden show hosted in 2023 at Mannheim, Bettina transformed several concrete driveways as a planting experiment on the former American military site, Spinelli Barracks. A wide median strip was cut in the middle, then long, linear gravel beds were installed and planted with a mix of stress-tolerant steppe, dry prairie, and native plants.

Within Hermannshof's habitat-themed plantings, Cassian created several complex and beautiful dry landscapes, including a Mediterranean garigue (top) and a dry limestone steppe (right) with salvia and euphorbia.

In 2001, Cassian created his first trial gravel gardens and called them "dry landscapes." He spread a 3-inch layer of 1/4- to 3/8-inch granite and porphyry gravel from a local quarry to test a new maintenance approach in a steppe-inspired planting. Sedum and yarrow, planted with a host of other perennials and grasses, are pictured here in summer and again in fall (top right and bottom right). Here, he changed from a conventional method of adding compost and providing regular irrigation to a more stress-based concept that mimics the natural conditions of a steppe landscape. The main factors include the absence of irrigation, fertilizers, and compost, mulching with stone or minerals rather than typical organic mulches like wood mulch or leaves, removing the organic plant remains from the site in late winter, and never cultivating the soil.

The North American Prairie Garden shines in full summer glory at Hermannshof. Butterfly milkweed, yellow coneflower, and Mexican feather grass feel right at home in the German gravel garden and bloom later in the season when many of the European natives have already finished flowering.

Gravel in American Public Gardens

OLBRICH BOTANICAL GARDENS
Madison, Wisconsin

Technique Trailblazer

Olbrich Botanical Gardens stands as a vanguard in sustainable gardening practices with four beautiful gravel gardens, including the Midwest's inaugural public gravel garden. Jeff Epping, retired horticulture director, spearheaded Olbrich's series of gravel gardens as a testament to its innovation since its inception in 2009. Over the years, the horticulture team has refined their techniques, conducted trials of various plants, and shared their knowledge with visitors from around the world.

"The gravel gardens fit with our overall efforts to be more sustainable," says Jeff. "We create more ecologically sound gardens by focusing on suitable plants and reducing the amount of water and chemicals we use."

In 2009, Jeff embarked on an experimental project, transforming a challenging, poorly drained area near the herb garden into both a rain garden and gravel garden. The transformation involved removing several aging arborvitaes and a dilapidated brick walkway. Soil from the rain garden was added to the adjacent gravel garden's soil and leveled. The perimeter was then edged with salvaged limestone and locally sourced boulders. Finally, 18 tons of 3⁄16-inch quartzite gravel filled the space. Since Jeff's inspiration came from plantsman Roy Diblik and his gravel garden, he enlisted Roy's help with the layout and installation of the garden's 700 plants. The horticulture team welcomed the opportunity to work with this garden legend despite their skepticism about his novel gardening technique.

Reflecting on her initial doubts, Samantha Peckham, current director of horticulture and a newcomer to the team at the time, admits, "I wasn't sure this was going to work, but I was completely wrong. From the very beginning, it just did beautifully and surpassed my expectations."

Today, the 730-square-foot garden flourishes in a purple sea of coneflowers, Russian sage, bee balm, ornamental onion, and prairie grasses that truly shine in the hottest days of summer. A gravel path leads through the long, narrow space to a seating area with two Adirondack chairs and accents of sea lavender and rattlesnake master.

"It's really cool to have people interact with these native plants that they may not see very often," says Avery Pronschinske, the horticulturist overseeing the gravel gardens, noting visitors can't miss the 8-foot, yellow-flowering prairie dock that lean into the walkways. "The gardens provide an opportunity for visitors to experience native plants close-up."

Convinced of gravel gardens' benefits, the horticulture team went on to create additional gravel gardens.

In 2012, a smaller, 1000-square-foot gravel garden was created near Olbrich's iconic Tower Garden with its 30-foot, prairie-style tower. While the Tower Garden was once home to a high-maintenance rose garden, the team has gradually phased out the chemically dependent rose varieties, added more drought-tolerant plants, and installed a rain garden with serpentine boardwalk. It's here where they added the gravel garden to further demonstrate water

OPPOSITE A vanguard in sustainable gardening, Olbrich is home to four gravel gardens, including some of the very first in the United States. At the entrance alongside the pyramidical Bolz Conservatory, this showcase gravel garden sets the tone for Olbrich's progressive style. "It really does an incredible job of introducing people to what they're going to experience inside, with all of its wildness, color, and diversity," says Samantha Peckham, director of horticulture.

Replacing a labor-intensive annual border just outside the fence, the third gravel garden welcomes visitors along the main road leading into Olbrich. No more thirsty, short-lived petunias and begonias. The 12-by-100-foot border is now filled with ornamental grasses and a mix of large, yellow daffodils for spring, and black-eyed Susan, yarrow, and coreopsis for summer. The gravel garden inspired the horticulture team to replace the adjacent lawn with a prairie dropseed meadow infused with drought-tolerant flowering perennials and bulbs, with additional color provided by self-seeding annuals.

conservation. They heavily planted it with prairie dropseed, calamint, and ornamental onion.

"One of the biggest benefits [of gravel gardens] is being able to highlight some of these native species that sometimes can go a little rogue in a traditional garden with more fertile soil," says Avery. "I fell in love with the gravel gardens just because of the diversity of native plants that shine in this deprived environment."

The third gravel garden, planted in 2010, replaced a labor-intensive annual border along the main road leading into Olbrich.

"This high-traffic area is the perfect spot for catching people's attention with lots of color," says Jeff. "While the annuals we planted there every year accomplished that, they were costly and required a lot of water, fertilizer, mulch, and labor compared to the gravel garden plants."

No more thirsty, short-lived petunias and begonias. The 12-by-100-foot border is now filled with ornamental grasses and a sunny perennial mix of large, yellow daffodils for spring and black-eyed Susan, yarrow, and coreopsis for summer. Simultaneously, the bordering lawn was replaced with a more sustainable meadow of 5000 prairie dropseed grasses. Both areas no longer need supplemental watering.

In 2014, the fourth and largest gravel garden (5000 square feet) was planted at Olbrich's entrance beside its 50-foot-high glass pyramidical Bolz Conservatory. The overgrown, 1970s-style landscape was removed, making way for a showcase gravel garden reflecting Olbrich's more progressive style.

"The garden is the focal point of the entrance," says Avery. "As guests enter, they see a constant flow of textures and colors that change through the seasons."

In spring, visitors are captivated by the garden's host of spring bulbs, including species tulips, daffodils, chionodoxa, and ornamental onions. In early summer, the show transitions to a kaleidoscope of colors and textures. The perennial mix includes purple beardtongue, yellow coreopsis, coneflowers in yellow and pink, white flowering spurge, brilliant orange butterfly milkweed, little bluestem, purple lead plant, white calamint, purple prairie clover, aster, and goldenrod. In late fall and winter, seed heads and grass plumes remain to provide habitat for overwintering insects, seeds to feed birds, and winter interest for visitors to enjoy.

"It really does an incredible job of introducing people to what they're going to experience inside, with all of its wildness, color, and diversity," says Samantha.

Olbrich's commitment to sustainability extends beyond gravel gardens. In the past twenty years, the team has replaced unused lawns with meadows, installed an underground cistern to collect rainwater, established three rain gardens, and redesigned landscape borders, replacing plants like

ABOVE Samantha Peckham (left), current director of horticulture, and Avery Pronschinske (right), the horticulturist overseeing the gravel gardens, are champions of the gravel garden technique. "It's really cool to have people interact with these native plants that they may not see very often," says Avery. "The gardens provide an opportunity for visitors to experience native plants close-up." **OPPOSITE** Silver eastern red cedar (*Juniperus virginiana* 'Glauca') grows to about 20 feet tall and has beautiful silvery-green needles and blue fruit that are ornamental and especially attractive to birds like cedar waxwings, song sparrows, and many others.

water-loving astilbe with Midwest natives and more site-appropriate plants. This dedication earned them the Garden Stewardship Award from the American Horticultural Society in 2022.

"We've been able to experiment with a new type of sustainable gardening and planting that has really proven to be truly more low-maintenance for us than traditional gardens," says Samantha.

Avery explains the biggest task with gravel gardens is the spring cleanup; it takes a day or two to cut back and haul out the past season's plant material. All collected material is placed in an area where the insects can emerge from the stems and leaves during the growing season. Toward fall, it is added to Olbrich's accelerated compost system. The only other task is occasional weeding or thinning of the garden's self-sowers that sometimes seed into crowns of neighboring plants or along the gravel gardens' edges. The established gardens don't require supplemental watering.

"In the seven years that I've been here, I've only watered the gravel gardens two times," says Avery. "That's a testament to how resilient they are even in drought seasons. They don't show signs of stress, which is amazing and impressive."

"I've learned a lot from these different gravel garden installations—which plants work well and which don't, and how to care for them in different settings," says Jeff. "It was a great learning experience and opportunity to share both the good and the bad with others to help them succeed."

Owned by the City of Madison, the 16-acre gardens continue to inspire city departments as more gravel gardens are planted in parking lot islands and parks and around municipal buildings, including the new City of Madison Parks Lakeside Offices complex.

"Don't be afraid to try new things like these gravel gardens," says Avery. "It's worth your while, and you never know—you might be completely surprised in the best possible way."

Updating an Established Gravel Garden

Once a gravel garden has been installed, the garden can be maintained as is or updated with the following touches:

SPRING SPECTACLE. Extend the gravel garden's seasonal beauty with a layer of spring bulbs. Bulbs thrive with this well-drained technique. Try daffodils, species tulips, alliums, or squill. Remember to plant them 4 to 6 inches deep in the soil beneath the gravel.

PLANT SHUFFLE. Over time, you may decide you want to adjust your plant layout. Maybe a plant grew too tall, or some are too dominant. Perhaps you've discovered a new plant that you want to add. Simply move gravel aside, carefully dig around the plant's roots, then lift the plant with a shovel. Replant it elsewhere, digging a deep hole and ensuring the roots touch the soil. Finally, cover around the crown of the plant with gravel again.

SELF-SOWING STARS. Embrace self-seeding plants like lanceleaf coreopsis (*Coreopsis lanceolata*), which sprout along the shallow edges of gravel gardens. Thin them out if needed, and even transplant some to other areas of your garden. Remember to water transplants until established.

BOLD AND BEAUTIFUL. Add one or two sculptural plants for a dramatic surprise. Popular choices include prairie dock (*Silphium terebinthinaceum*), Adam's needle (*Yucca filamentosa*), tall moor grass (*Molinia arundinacea* 'Skyracer'), rattlesnake master (*Eryngium yuccifolium*), and giant coneflower (*Rudbeckia maxima*).

POLLINATOR PARADISE. Aim for a long, gapless season of flowering plants from early spring to late fall to ensure pollen and nectar for pollinators. A few season extenders include bulbs for spring, then aster and goldenrod for fall. Olbrich's gravel gardens are home to the rusty patched bumble bee (*Bombus affinis*)—one of three federally endangered bee species in the United States.

ABOVE As in any garden, some plants in the gravel garden do better than others. If some begin to become too dominant and crowd less-competitive plants out over time, a little refereeing is in order to restore a nice balance. Preserving plant diversity maintains visual appeal and provides the best habitat for insects, birds, and other creatures that live in the garden.

OPPOSITE: TOP ROW Carthusian pink (*Dianthus carthusianorum*) and lanceleaf coreopsis (*Coreopsis lanceolata*) are beautiful additions to the garden and are happiest in dry soils, so much so that they often self-seed in nooks and crannies and sometimes crowns of surrounding plants. It is best to select those to keep or remove in spring when seedlings are most visible and easy to pull. BOTTOM ROW Adam's needle (*Yucca filamentosa*) and giant coneflower (*Rudbeckia maxima*) are stately sculptural plants that add interest and drama to the garden.

❶ **Tennessee coneflower** (*Echinacea tennesseensis*) provides food for a hungry rabbit. Many plants can support some munching from animals after they are well established but may need to be protected for a year or two until they grow large enough to tolerate it. ❷ **Flowering spurge** (*Euphorbia corollata*) is also known as prairie baby's breath for its beautiful white, airy sprays of flowers in late summer. Don't let its beauty fool you—it's one of the toughest plants in the gravel garden and even reseeds in the open gravel from time to time. ❸ **'Summer Beauty' ornamental onion** (*Allium lusitanicum* 'Summer Beauty') has clean, dark green foliage all season long and often flowers for two full months in mid- to late summer, which this honey bee is enjoying. Like all alliums, animals find the foliage and bulbs distasteful. ❹ **Globe thistle** (*Echinops ritro*) has showy, steely-blue, ping-pong-size blooms that attract pollinators and last well as cut flowers. The plant requires dry soils, so it thrives in gravel. ❺ **Yellow coneflower** (*Echinacea paradoxa*) is a beacon in the landscape with its 3-foot-tall, rich yellow flowers that appear in early summer. The seed heads are highly ornamental and goldfinches feast on the seeds all winter long. Interestingly, this is the only yellow coneflower species and is used in breeding programs to produce orange and red coneflower cultivars. ❻ **Rattlesnake master** (*Eryngium yuccifolium*) is a highly architectural perennial for any garden. This native is short-lived but persists in prairies through self-seeding, which it does very effectively. If it doesn't reseed in your garden, it will need to be replanted from time to time. ❼ **Tickseed** (*Coreopsis palmata*) is a nice addition to the gravel garden for its brilliant gold flowers in late spring. It moderately spreads by rhizomes in the loose gravel but is easily managed by gently pulling the running stems from the perimeter of the plant in early spring. ❽ **'Pocahontas' beardtongue** (*Penstemon digitalis* 'Pocahontas') is a showy burgundy-foliaged cultivar with light pink blossoms in mid-spring and showy seed heads for the rest of the season. ❾ **Butterfly milkweed** (*Asclepias tuberosa*) is the longest-lived, most easily managed milkweed species. It is difficult to transplant, but once established is very long-lived. Of course, its foliage is essential to monarch butterfly caterpillars, and many adult butterfly species feed on its nectar.

RIGHT Hoary vervain (*Verbena stricta*) sets forth gorgeous vertical lavender flower spires that grace the garden for four to six weeks beginning in July. Bees and butterflies visit the flowers, and the leaves are a host food for common buckeye caterpillars.

LEFT If you take a little time to observe life in your gravel garden, you often see wonderful creatures like this bluet damselfly resting on the flower buds of our native nodding onion (*Allium cernuum*).

The four gravel gardens at Olbrich demonstrate the variations in style and applications for this innovative gardening technique. Featured here are (1) the 5000-square-foot entry garden (above), (2) a simple and intimate gravel garden near a rain garden to further demonstrate water conservation (right) (3) the first gravel garden created in conjunction with Roy Diblik in 2009 (opposite top) and (4) the former annual-border-turned-gravel-garden along the main road into Olbrich (opposite bottom).

ABOVE

OLBRICH
BOTANICAL
GARDENS
HORTICULTURE

"One of the biggest benefits [of gravel gardens] is being able to highlight some of these native species that sometimes can go a little rogue in a traditional garden with more fertile soil," says Avery. "I fell in love with the gravel gardens just because of the diversity of native plants that shine in this deprived environment." Learn more and find full plant lists at www.olbrich.org.

MEADOWBROOK FARM
Jenkintown, Pennsylvania

Resilient Beauty

Meadowbrook Farm's gravel gardens, curated by head gardener Glenn Ashton, are a testament to the historic estate's legacy of creativity and unconventional gardening. These intriguing gardens, showcased within the entry parking lots, defy expectations with their bold plant selections. Here, tree-form yuccas and prickly chollas, more commonly associated with the deserts of Arizona, make a striking visual impact. Silhouettes of yucca and prickly pears stand out amid drifts of baby's breath, pine-leaved penstemon, and pink hummingbird mint with accents of globe thistle and brilliant yellow Texas primrose. The warm, earthen tones of the rock border and gravel provide a contrasting backdrop.

The inception of these gravel gardens in 2008 was a direct result of Glenn's innovative thinking. After a deer fence was installed on the property, Glenn was tasked with relocating a patch of prickly pear cacti to make way for the new fence. He embraced this opportunity to create something unique. Taking inspiration from an alpine garden at John Marano's family nursery in Fort Washington, Pennsylvania, Glenn expanded the planting by creating a gravel island on the high side of the parking lot.

He repurposed pallets of boulders from a remodeled display garden and artfully arranged a 2-foot-high wall backfilled with dark gravel from the parking lot. His goal was to create dry, fast-draining conditions. "I wanted to create these environments where water just sheds through rapidly," says Glenn.

His fascination with water began at a young age. "I loved watching storms roll in and would roll up the garage door to see where all the rainwater would go." His early gardening experiences with his dad and his childhood collection of used garden books further fueled his passion for plants.

"I always wanted to grow whatever I wanted to grow, and if the plant required sharp drainage, and I didn't have it, then I needed to create it," he says.

Glenn planted the gravel garden with the original prickly pears, along with other hardy arid species like beaked yucca and cholla, then filled in with desert perennials. Using a crowbar, he lifted rocks and wedged a plant's roots into the crevices, packing in a little soil before gently lowering the crowbar and replacing the rocks. "You just have to be careful the rock doesn't come crashing down on your fingers," he notes. Some plants are planted in sheer gravel, while others are planted in bowls of a gravely soil mix.

"It's just a totally different style of gardening, and I'm fascinated with the diversity of plants," says Glenn. "And the beautiful thing is you don't have to worry about going around watering." However, he does water new plants until they're established.

To protect marginally hardy cacti during the winter when the garden is closed, Glenn covers them with white plastic trash cans that have vent holes cut in their sides. "Wet and cold are the death knell of these marginally hardy Southwestern plants where they only get 12 inches of rainfall each year," says Glenn. His one caution about using trash can cloches is critters might make winter homes in these dry environments and feast on plant roots. To deter them, he uses a granular repellent. In his parents' garden, he creates aesthetic cloches of 3-gallon glass

OPPOSITE Meadowbrook's fabulously original gravel gardens continue this historic garden's legacy for creative spectacles. Here at the parking lot entrance, the gravel garden border intrigues with its bold plant combinations and artistic rock walls.

Silhouettes of yucca and prickly pears stand out amid drifts of baby's breath, pine-leaved penstemon, and pink hummingbird mint with accents of globe thistle and brilliant yellow Texas primrose.

jars with bottoms cut out and cork tops added to release heat and moisture.

Beyond the original gravel garden, he has created two more gravel gardens and experimented with other fast-draining garden projects, including alpine troughs and a restored dry-laid stone wall. Glenn installed a series of troughs on pedestals in one of the gardens around the estate house three years ago. He also transformed a 6-foot dry stack wall, located in a neglected back courtyard where a toolshed once stood. He saw potential in this "no man's land," reimagining it into a stunning stone-walled garden with cascading cotoneaster, wispy Mexican feather grasses that dance in the slightest breeze, and spurge and irises peeking from pockets along the rock wall.

"I just love it because it gives a different perspective," says Glenn. "It's already 4 feet off the ground, so things like miniature iris are right in front of your face."

Glenn's visionary work at Meadowbrook Farm continues the legacy left by J. Liddon Pennock Jr., who bequeathed the 25-acre property to the Pennsylvania Horticultural Society in 2004. Mr. Pennock, a professional florist and avid gardener known for his eccentricity, was famous for pushing boundaries in gardening and floral design. He forced flowers into bloom for his extravagant designs for the Philadelphia Flower Show. He also decorated the Nixon White House at Christmas and arranged the flowers for Tricia Nixon's White House wedding. His artistic mastery extended to his extraordinary home garden at Meadowbrook where he planted spectacular flower beds, espaliered a southern magnolia along a warm stone wall, and cloud-pruned two weeping hemlocks around the garden's signature eagle sculpture.

Today, the creativity fostered by Mr. Pennock's legacy continues at Meadowbrook, where Glenn and his team reimagine its nineteen distinct gardens each year, highlighting seasonal interest and spectacular plantings throughout the property. The fabulously original gravel gardens are the perfect homage to this legacy.

ABOVE Tree cholla (*Cylindropuntia imbricata* var. *arborescens*) is native to the southwestern United States and needs excellent drainage to survive. Glenn planted it on several feet of pure washed gravel. OPPOSITE Head gardener Glenn Ashton started his first gravel garden with prickly pear in an island of gravel mix and kept experimenting with more plants that thrived with only the rainfall they received. But most required good drainage, which was a challenge to create. "I wanted to create these environments where water just sheds through rapidly," he says.

Gravel Gardening in Troughs

Troughs are a great place to get started with gravel gardens, especially if you don't have room for a full gravel garden. They're an easy way to experiment without a big investment. Plus, you can observe the plants close-up. Once you've mastered gravel gardening in one trough, you'll find you want more troughs or even a full gravel garden.

CONTAINER: First, choose a porous container with holes in the bottom. We prefer terra-cotta pots or hypertufa troughs made of cement, peat moss, and perlite that mimics the look of natural stone.

PLANTS: Select succulents, cacti, and alpine plants that thrive in well-draining soil. A few favorites include hens and chicks, sedums, and hedgehog cacti.

ASSEMBLE: Fill the base of the container with a gravelly mix. We suggest 1 part potting soil with 2 parts pea gravel. Next, place the plants in the container. Add more gravel mix around the plants. Finish the trough with a top dressing of fine gravel, accented with decorative rocks. Further experiment with planting between rock crevices, which many alpine and desert plants prefer.

CARE: Place troughs in full sun where you can enjoy them. Since the containers have a limited amount of soil beneath the gravel layer, unlike a gravel garden in natural earth, they will need some supplemental watering, especially during the heat of summer.

ABOVE Glenn is displaying beautiful troughs with creative combinations amid a lawn where visitors can walk around them to get a close view of the diminutive plantings.

OPPOSITE: TOP ROW Troughs are a great way to experiment with gravel gardening on a smaller, easily observable scale. Trough favorites include hens and chicks (*Sempervivum*), sedums, and variety of low-growing alpines. BOTTOM ROW Experiment with growing plants that drape over walls, like flowered 'Herrenhausen' ornamental oregano (*Origanum laevigatum* 'Herrenhausen') (left). You can also try planting in crevices in walls. Try hens and chicks like marjoram (*Origanum libanoticum*) (top right) and 'Gold Nugget' (*Sempervivum*) (bottom right).

Rugged Desert Darlings

❶ **Partridge feather** (*Tanacetum densum* ssp. *amani*), native to the mountains of Turkey, is quite at home here growing in gravel. Its wonderful silver fuzzy leaves and stems only reach 3 to 5 inches tall, with vividly contrasting gold flowers in early summer. ❷ **Bear's breeches** (*Acanthus spinosus*) is architecturally bold in both foliage and flower and well-suited to growing in gravel. Its classical look was the inspiration for the Corinthian leaf motif in ancient Greek and Roman art. ❸ **'Durango Spineless' beavertail cactus** (*Opuntia basilaris* 'Durango Spineless') is a low-growing cultivar with soothing, blue-green, wafer-like spineless pads. ❹ **'Bristol Fairy' baby's breath** (*Gypsophila paniculata* 'Bristol Fairy') and its delicate white flower sprays complement almost every plant in the garden. ❺ **'Sapphire Skies' beaked yucca** (*Yucca rostrata* 'Sapphire Skies'), when young, must be covered in winter in the moist climate of the Northeast, not to protect them from the cold but from rain that can cause rotting. As the yuccas age and produce more foliage, they no longer need to be sheltered in winter. ❻ **'Georgia Pancake' fringed blue star** (*Amsonia ciliata* var. *tenuifolia* 'Georgia Pancake') is a short-growing cultivar, only reaching about 6 inches in height. Glenn planted it atop a wall where visitors can appreciate its fine-textured foliage that cascades over the edges of the stone. ❼ **Ladybird® Sunglow Texas primrose** (*Calylophus* hybrid 'WNCYLASUN', Ladybird® Sunglow) is a very floriferous hybrid of this Southwest native gem. ❽ **'Herrenhausen' ornamental oregano** (*Origanum laevigatum* 'Herrenhausen') feeds a hungry western bee in the garden. ❾ **Pincushion cactus** (*Coryphantha vivipara*) is a hardy cactus that grows in the central United States from Texas to Canada, where it thrives in rocky sites and sand prairies.

ABOVE For the winter months, Glenn moves century agaves from the gravel garden into Meadowbrook's greenhouses. **LEFT** Great globe thistle (*Echinops sphaerocephalus*) makes a bold statement in the garden as it towers above surrounding perennials.

Glenn embraces the showy, hot-colored blooms of these xeric plants, including (clockwise from top left) royal catchfly (*Silene regia*), hummingbird trumpet (*Zauschneria garrettii*), Brakelights® redflower false yucca (*Hesperaloe parviflora* 'Perpa', Brakelights®), and 'Queen Nectarine' hummingbird mint (*Agastache* 'Queen Nectarine'), as well as the straight species whose flowers tower over him (opposite).

Glenn transformed a neglected courtyard's 6-foot, dry stack wall into a stunning reimagined garden. The fast-draining space now features Mexican feather grass (*Nassella tenuissima*), golden oats (*Stipa gigantea*), 'Streibs Findling' bearberry cotoneaster (*Cotoneaster dammeri* 'Streibs Findling'), Russian sage (*Perovskia atriplicifolia*), myrtle spurge (*Euphorbia myrsinites*), and 'Pancake' creeping juniper (*Juniperus horizontalis* 'Pancake'). Learn more at www.phsonline.org/locations/phs-meadowbrook-farm.

CHANTICLEER GARDEN
Wayne, Pennsylvania

Creative Masterpiece

Nestled along a slope at Chanticleer Garden, just outside Philadelphia, lies a hidden gem: a highly imaginative gravel garden. This horticulture wonderland showcases sculptural yuccas and agaves standing dramatically among familiar prairie plants and more exotic Mediterranean species.

Lisa Roper, the horticulturist who manages this garden, thrives on creative challenges. Over her thirty-five-year career at Chanticleer, she played a crucial role in shaping the gardens before they opened to the public in 1993. She contributed to a wildflower wonderland in the Asian Woods for ten years, then took on the rock-walled Ruin Garden and nearby gravel garden in 2013.

"I love creating this garden to transport visitors to hot and dry California or Colorado," says Lisa about the distinctive gravel garden. "It's so exotic and definitely not the vernacular of lush Pennsylvania."

Unlike many low-maintenance gravel gardens that use a thick layer of soilless gravel, this garden features soil mixed with gravel then topped with fine gravel. The design aim is to replicate an arid Mediterranean environment.

"The plants self-sow with abundance here," explains Lisa. "This randomness, combined with a careful repetition of strategically placed plants, creates a natural feeling to the garden."

Originally designed by horticulturist Laurel Voran and previous Chanticleer director Chris Woods in 2000, the gravel garden was planted on a south-facing slope with huge granite curbstone steps cascading to an arbor. When Laurel passed the baton to Lisa, she took a year to observe and envision enhancements.

"It's a strong garden, so I just watched the first year to see where I could improve," she says. The following year, she removed aggressive plants like big bluestem that obstructed views and introduced bold, broad-leafed, silvery plants such as silver sage and sea kale.

"I think about it as designing by subtraction," Lisa says of her editing process. Drawing on her art school background, she seeks balance among plantings and draws design inspiration from nature.

"Less is often more," she notes, emphasizing the need for negative space around focal plants, when filler plants like scabiosa and orlaya threaten to obscure them.

After clearing the clutter, Lisa introduces architectural statement plants among finer foliage. She favors hardy, sculptural succulents like beaked yucca, nodding yucca, Parry's agave, and beavertail cactus.

The garden's management comes with its challenges. One major ongoing task is managing the level of self-sowing.

"This is a commitment garden," Lisa says. Both weeds and desirable plants like Mediterranean spurge and moon carrot self-sow prolifically. She discerns the difference among the two and manages desirable "volunteers" through rigorous thinning and deadheading.

Navigating drought conditions is another challenge. Lisa does not water established plants, since this is a designated xeriscape demonstration garden. To cope with the water restrictions, she bare-roots plants—removing all soil before planting—to get their roots in contact with the soil and help them

OPPOSITE Chanticleer's highly imaginative gravel garden resembles the aesthetic of an arid Mediterranean landscape and artfully curates plantings to create a horticultural wonderland. Pure white spires of 'Floristan White' blazing star (*Liatris spicata* 'Floristan Weiss') dance along the bluestone walkway near the Ruin Garden.

Set on a south-facing slope, huge granite curbstone steps let visitors comfortably explore every corner of the garden. The gravel garden features highly architectural plants including hardy, sculptural succulents and stately columnar junipers.

acclimate more quickly. Last year, during a prolonged spring drought, she had to spot-water new plants for six weeks, learning to plant only when rain is forecasted and to favor more resilient species.

Despite these challenges, the gravel garden continues to thrive and evolve, a testament to Lisa's artistic vision and plant expertise. She attributes her inspiration to Chanticleer's high artistic standards and the creative energy of her seven fellow horticulturists.

"Our director, Bill Thomas, is always saying 'you know the bar is up and we need to do better,'" she says. "The creative ferment from my co-workers inspires me." The design process is a conversation with Bill; he supports experimentation and following their own vision.

Forever the editor, Lisa looks to introduce new plants or replace plants that died out.

"I'm looking at repetition in the garden to hold it together but also looking for accents and surprise," she says. "I want to grow lots of wonderful things."

In early spring, clusters of dainty, dwarf bulbous irises emerge in purple and blue drifts against a backdrop of Mexican feather grass with its wispy, tan foliage from the previous fall. "It's a great companion plant for the earliest bulbs and moves with the slightest breeze," Lisa notes.

By late May, the garden features large ivory allium spheres mingling with purple and orange ice plants, silver sage's fuzzy leaves, and the bell-shaped flowers of 'Blue Ribbons' clematis.

The spring show continues into June with a "white moment," where delicate orlaya weaves among silver sage, 'Kintzley's Ghost' honeysuckle, and a potted cereus cactus with stunning nightly blooms.

In the summer, the garden shines with Tennessee purple coneflower, 'Karl Foerster' feather reed grass, prairie blazing star, blue thistlelike sea holly, and Peruvian feather grass. "These grasses are wonderful when backlit. They prefer good air circulation, so don't let taller plants overwhelm them," Lisa advises.

The fall season culminates with broad sweeps of 'Raydon's Favorite' aromatic aster, 'Summer Breeze' gaura with its dainty pale pink blooms, and Korean feather grass with its showy, pink plumes.

ABOVE With its narrow vertical form, 'Taylor' eastern red cedar (*Juniperus virginiana* 'Taylor') adds formality to the free-flowing perennial plantings of the gravel garden. OPPOSITE Lisa Roper masterfully cares for the garden. "This is a commitment garden," she says. Both weeds and desirable plants like Mediterranean spurge and moon carrot self-sow prolifically. She discerns the difference among the two and manages desirable "volunteers" through rigorous thinning and deadheading.

ABOVE When a tulip poplar fell in a once-shaded seating area, Lisa swapped in sun-loving silvery plants to surround the stone furnishings. **RIGHT** She chose low-growing ones to allow views into the gravel garden. The unique white flower umbels of moon carrot (*Seseli gummiferum*) seem to gravitate above the plantings. **OPPOSITE** "I'm looking at repetition in the garden to hold it together but also looking for accents and surprise," says Lisa. "I want to grow lots of wonderful things." Witness the foliage of soaptree yucca (*Yucca elata*) in a tapestry of fine-textured foliage and flowers.

❶ **American century plant** (*Agave americana*) is native to the U.S. Southwest and Mexico and has very stately heavy foliage—each leaf with a prominent sharp spine at the tip. Lisa digs each plant in the fall and overwinters them in the garden's temperate glasshouse. ❷ **'Kintzley's Ghost grape honeysuckle** (*Lonicera reticulata* 'Kintzley's Ghost') features uniquely shaped, clasping, silvery leaves that glow in the morning sun. ❸ **Variegated foxtail agave** (*Agave attenuata* 'Variegata') and its yellow-edged leaves shimmer in the morning light. This agave, like all the others in the garden, are overwintered in a cool greenhouse. ❹ **Mexican hens and chicks hybrid** (*Echeveria* × *gigantea*) is a nonhardy succulent that is grown in decorative troughs throughout the garden. ❺ Lisa has found the best mix for optimum draining is to combine pea gravel (⅓-inch) and a similar-size sharp gravel together (both locally sourced) with the top 6 to 8 inches of existing soil in the garden. She then tops off the planting bed with about an inch of the pure gravel mixture after planting. ❻ **Mediterranean spurge** (*Euphorbia characias* ssp. *wulfenii*) thrives in the well-drained soil and even reseeds, which is never a bad thing with such a beautiful plant. ❼ **Moon carrot** (*Seseli gummiferum*) is a biennial or short-lived perennial that is an absolute standout in the garden with its fantastic architectural form, ferny silver-gray foliage, and unusual umbelliferous flowers. ❽ **'Blue Glitter' sea holly** (*Eryngium planum* 'Blaukappe') features blue-gray spiny foliage and blue flowers that stand 2 to 3 feet tall in the garden. It is notoriously difficult to transplant but well worth the effort. ❾ **Lavender cotton** (*Santolina chamaecyparissus*), hardy in Lisa's garden, sports brilliant yellow button-like flowers in summer which contrast nicely against the silvery aromatic evergreen foliage. ❿ **'Beavertail' cactus** (*Opuntia basilaris* 'Beavertail') and Mediterranean spurge (*Euphorbia characias* ssp. *wulfenii*) make a stunning combination planted side by side. ⓫ Seen again here, **'Kintzley's Ghost grape honeysuckle** (*Lonicera reticulata* 'Kintzley's Ghost') stands about 6 feet tall and wide in the garden. This cultivar was originally propagated in the 1880s by William Kintzley at Iowa State University. It was

lost in commerce, then rediscovered at a relative's home in Fort Collins, Colorado. 12 **'Elijah Blue' fescue** (*Festuca glauca* 'Elijah Blue') and its fine-textured, silvery-blue foliage adds a sense of airiness and delightfully softens the hard lines of the hypertufa troughs. Lisa has found that this cultivar readily reseeds in the gravelly soil.

The iconic 'Sapphire Skies' beaked yucca (*Yucca rostrata* 'Sapphire Skies') was planted from seed collected by Colorado horticulturist Lauren Springer in 2002 and now towers over this peaceful area on the edge of the gravel garden where you can sit on a stone bench overlooking the garden and admire its beauty. **OPPOSITE** Troughs planted in the nearby Ruin Garden repeat the gravel garden's plants to connect the two spaces. Lisa says troughs are an easy way to experiment with gravel gardens. Featured here are mountain aloe (*Aloe marlothii*) and 'Afterglow' Mexican hens and chicks (*Echeveria* 'Afterglow') (top left), Mexican hens and chicks hybrid (*Echeveria* x *gigantea*) and Madagascar ocotillo (*Alluaudia procera*) (top right), blue myrtle cactus (*Myrtillocactus geometrizans*) (bottom left), and red pencil tree (*Euphorbia tirucalli*) and propeller plant (*Crassula perfoliata* var. *falcata*) (bottom right).

Bulbs in the Gravel Layer

Bulbs thrive in well-draining soil, making a sloped gravel garden an ideal environment for them. Lisa has found that even tulips can become more perennial in gravelly soil, often lasting years. Some of her favorites include reticulated iris, triplet lilies, small-flowered daffodils, tulips, grape hyacinth, and ornamental onion. Here are her tips for bulb care for the gravel garden:

PLANT DEEPLY. Plant bulbs twice the usual depth (three times the depth of the bulb) to ensure good bulb and root development.

DETER PESTS. When planting, sprinkle blood meal around bulbs to keep rodents away.

EDIT EXISTING BULBS. Over time, the colors in a bulb mix can become muddled. Lisa, a skilled photographer, often takes photos of her bulb display to help with her editing decisions.

TEST NEW VARIETIES. Start with a handful of bulbs to see how they perform. If they do well, snip blooms and move them about the garden to find the best combinations for planting more the next year.

HIDE FADING FOLIAGE. Pair bulbs with late-season perennials, like asters, to mask the fading foliage.

PLANT FOR IMPACT. Arrange bulbs in drifts and pockets along slopes or throughout the garden. Small bulbs, such as muscari, should be planted in large quantities for a significant effect, while larger bulbs, like allium, can be used as accents in smaller groups scattered throughout.

ABOVE LEFT Tulips thrive in the gravel layer and can even become more perennial with the excellent drainage. Lisa creates this stunning combination with 'Orange Emperor' tulip (*Tulipa* 'Orange Emperor'), 'Hawera' daffodil (*Narcissus* 'Hawera'), grape hyacinth (*Muscari armeniacum*), and 'Valerie Finnis' grape hyacinth (*Muscari armeniacum* 'Valerie Finnis'). ABOVE RIGHT A lovely silver and blue combination in early spring features 'Queen Fabiola' triplet lily (*Triteleia* 'Queen Fabiola'), 'Powis Castle' wormwood (*Artemisia* 'Powis Castle'), and silver sage (*Salvia argentea*).

RIGHT Lisa created another stunning combination with 'Ivory Queen' ornamental onion (*Allium karataviense* 'Ivory Queen'), Table Mountain® ice plant (*Delosperma* 'John Proffitt'), Granita Orange® ice plant (*Delosperma* 'John PJS02S'), and Sunsparkler® 'Plum Dazzled' stonecrop (*Sedum rupestre* 'Plum Dazzled'). **BELOW RIGHT** 'Rudy' triplet lily (*Triteleia* 'Rudy') shines with the soft developing flower sprays of Mexican feather grass (*Nassella tenuissima*).

LEFT 'Queen Fabiola' triplet lily (*Triteleia* 'Queen Fabiola') partners well with 'Solar Fire' ursinia (*Ursinia anthemoides* 'Solar Fire').

"Editing is an integral part of having a wild garden," says Lisa. "For the garden to feel naturalistic, it should have repetition from aggressive seeders like asters and poppy mallows, but they can't take over." Featured here are 'Ivory Queen' ornamental onion (*Allium karataviense* 'Ivory Queen'), Table Mountain® ice plant (*Delosperma* 'John Proffitt'), and Sunsparkler® 'Plum Dazzled' stonecrop (*Sedum rupestre* 'Plum Dazzled') as well as the upright flowers of king's spear (*Asphodeline lutea*) and wider sprays of silver sage (*Salvia argentea*). Learn more and find full plant lists at www.chanticleergarden.org.

REIMAN GARDENS at IOWA STATE UNIVERSITY
Ames, Iowa

Terraced Showcase

Reiman Gardens' plans for an elaborate terraced hillside garden sounded like a good idea at the time. However, in 2015 when Ed Lyon became the garden's new director, he proposed a more sustainable approach. A longtime environmental advocate, Ed encouraged the team to reconsider the water-intensive Hanging Gardens of Babylon–style garden and adopt a more ecological gravel garden for the hillside. He had been involved with other horticulturists in Wisconsin exploring this new gardening method and had already built one in the garden he just left. Luckily the team agreed, and today, the 1-acre Hillside Water-wise Garden is a sustainable showpiece.

A grand staircase climbs 35 limestone steps up the hillside to a beautiful gazebo with impressive views of the Reiman Gardens conservatory and surrounding gardens as well as borrowed views of Iowa State University's football stadium. A winding path cuts through four terraces, each with uniquely themed gravel gardens. The lowest level features a rainwater gravel garden brimming with water-loving plants like hardy hibiscus, black-eyed Susan, sneezeweed, turtlehead, and cardinal flower. Ascending a level, the next gravel garden pays tribute to the Dutch Wave design style, featuring salvia, allium, lamb's ears, and catmint. The next level, an ornamental gravel garden, features tough, drought-tolerant perennials like amsonia, joe-pye weed, calamint, yarrow, little bluestem, and anise hyssop. Finally, the top terrace displays high plains plants like spurge, sedum, dianthus, blue grama grass, and gaura—all adaptive to low water and fertility needs.

Ed came to Reiman Gardens with experience in gravel gardens and a big heart for education. Inspired by earlier gravel gardens by Roy Diblik and Jeff Epping, he installed his first gravel garden at the Allen Centennial Garden on the campus of the University of Wisconsin-Madison in 2013. He was eager to promote the concept's water-use efficiency and relatively low maintenance. He converted a former bog garden that had a leaky liner and had become a "giant weed patch." Ed and his team of student interns cleaned out plants and a rubber liner to discover a sandy bottom, ideal for a gravel garden. He secured funding through a grant to install a boardwalk and three themed gardens—a rain garden, a meadow, and a xeriscape-style gravel garden. In the process, he learned some key lessons to carry forward in his next gravel garden project. Among them included the weight of gravel and challenge in transporting it, how to best dig holes for plant installations, and how to get the gravel evenly spread to avoid shallow areas vulnerable to weeds. He also learned the importance of removing the upper surface of potting soil around new plants to prevent weed seeds from sprouting later.

"I call it low-impact gardening," says Ed. "It's low-impact on the environment because you use dramatically less water, less chemicals, and less fertilizers. In addition, it is low-impact physically on the body, with less maintenance and labor."

When Ed moved to Reiman Gardens in 2015, he was impressed with the 17-acre gardens known for their renowned Dr. Griffith Buck rose collection, trial gardens, prairie-style architecture, and of course, Elwood—the world's largest concrete gnome that stands 15 feet tall and weighs 3500 pounds.

OPPOSITE The 1-acre Hillside Water-wise Garden is a sustainable showpiece at Reiman Gardens. A grand staircase climbs 35 limestone steps up the hillside to a beautiful gazebo with impressive views of the conservatory and surrounding gardens.

A winding path cuts through four terraces, each with a uniquely themed gravel garden. The lowest level features a rainwater gravel garden brimming with water-loving plants like hardy hibiscus, joe-pye weed, sneezeweed, turtlehead, and cardinal flower. Ascending a level, the next gravel garden pays tribute to the Dutch Wave design style featuring salvia, ornamental onion, lamb's ears, and catmint. The next level, an ornamental gravel garden, features tough, drought-tolerant perennials like amsonia, black-eyed Susan, calamint, yarrow, little bluestem, and anise hyssop. Finally, the top terrace displays high plains plants like spurge, sedum, dianthus, blue grama grass, and gaura--all adapted to low water and fertility needs.

Ed's first project was implementing the plan for the hillside gardens. He started by working with Iowa State's facilities team to survey the site and translate the master plan into a working plan. The university contracted the excavation work and building of the stacked stone walls. A winding path with a less than 5 percent slope was created for accessibility.

"Since the stairs and walls were pretty formal, I wanted the path edges to wave and curve into the garden beds for a more natural effect," he says.

Once in place, Ed and his team contributed to the installation. They commissioned a regional steel fabricating company to design custom handrails with rootlike bases apropos for a garden railing. Next, they added 18 inches of amended soil since the site had been stripped of its topsoil.

The gravel posed several challenges. First, they needed a lot—200 tons for the required 4- to 6-inch layer across the 1-acre site. While they tried to find a local source, the closest were in adjoining states. They considered substituting local pea gravel for the quartzite gravel but were concerned the rounded stones wouldn't be as effective in creating the essential pore space to prevent weed germination. They ended up choosing quartzite gravel, since it worked so well in Ed's previous gravel garden project, and sourced it from South Dakota. While the gravel was relatively cheap (less than $30 per ton), the $10,000 shipping fee dramatically increased the overall cost.

The next obstacle was distributing the gravel across the 1-acre, sloped site. Wheelbarrowing the gravel was a daunting task that would have physically taxed the staff and volunteers. A team member suggested a boom truck, typically used to pump concrete, to handle the gravel. To everyone's relief, this method proved effective, and the boom truck was hired to deliver 210 tons of gravel throughout the terraced garden. However, the team was taken aback by the gravel's color. Ed, expecting gray gravel similar to what he had used in Wisconsin, was surprised to find that the South Dakota gravel had a distinct pink hue.

"Oh my God, we just made a giant pink gravel garden," Ed told horticulture director Sarah Rummery as they looked up the hillside of newly spread gravel. "It was a bit of a shock at first, but the color gradually dulled and was less noticeable as the plants filled in."

They added a wide mix of plants for each of the themed areas and were delighted by how quickly the plants established and performed in the gravel.

In 2019, the gravel garden that they named the Hillside Water-wise Garden was one of 21 gardens featured in the U.S. Botanic Garden's exhibit "Celebrating New American Gardens" in Washington, D.C.

Today, the terraced garden is the perfect backdrop for two annual events, including the Spirits in the Garden with hundreds of carved jack-o'-lanterns displayed along the garden's walls, and Winter Wonderscape with a holiday light show projected on the garden's facade.

"A gravel garden is a great choice for public gardens to demonstrate future solutions for gardening in a changing climate," says Ed, who retired in 2024 and leaves a legacy with his sustainable gardening practices. "And the Midwest is the perfect place to try one, since it's home to the widest range of conditions in the country, with 95-degree temps and 95 percent humidity in summer to 30 degrees below zero and no humidity in winter."

OPPOSITE Horticulturist Kara Hetrick tends to the gravel gardens and says, "My favorite thing about gravel gardens is that they tend to care for themselves, and if you select the right plants, they rarely need supplemental watering, and the plants stay nice and tidy!"

Elements of a Demonstration Garden

Creating a demonstration garden is an excellent way to showcase sustainable practices, innovative techniques, or aesthetic designs to a broader audience. Through experiential learning, visitors can learn about different plants, new growing methods, and care tips. Ed has created a number of demonstration gardens and offers these tips:

PURPOSE: Start by defining the garden's purpose, then develop a theme, whether promoting native plants, introducing a new design style, or offering water-wise gardening techniques. Thematic areas make it easier for visitors to see, understand, and appreciate different gardening design concepts. They also demonstrate that plants do best grouped with other plants that thrive in similar conditions.

MAP: Post a map identifying key garden elements and explain their purpose and how they relate to the overall design.

SIGNAGE: Add signage and plant labels to provide valuable information about the plants, techniques, or practices being demonstrated. For a gravel garden, include information about the gravel layer, garden maintenance, and ecological benefits. Alternatively, informational brochures can be made available in a protected box, or a QR code can be displayed to link visitors to related digital content.

ACCESSIBILITY: Ensure the garden is accessible to everyone. Design wide, even pathways and include raised beds or other accessible features if needed. In Reiman Gardens' gravel garden, concrete paths with a less than 5 percent slope easily wind through the space and allow visitors of all abilities to use the space equally.

EVENTS: Host garden tours and workshops in the garden to share your expertise. These can even be volunteer working events such as a fall cutback or bulb planting in the gravel garden.

AESTHETICS: Design plays an important role in engaging visitors. Think about the use of color, texture, and layers. At Reiman Gardens, Ed organized the gravel garden tiers with different garden themes, including rainwater control, ornamental beauty, Dutch Wave sustainability, and alpine planting.

ABOVE Be clear as to the intent of the garden.

OPPOSITE: TOP ROW Design sidewalks to gradually traverse the garden at a grade of 5 percent or less to be sure it is accessible to all garden visitors. Offer benches for people to rest as they navigate and enjoy the garden. BOTTOM LEFT Engage visitors with clever plant tags like this lamb-shaped one for lamb's ears. BOTTOM RIGHT Use QR codes to provide more detailed information on plants like this joe-pye weed (*Eutrochium maculatum*).

Lamb's Ear
Stachys byzantina

Plant of Interest
4

Water-wise Winners

❶ **'Matrona' stonecrop** (*Hylotelephium* 'Matrona') and 'Munstead' English lavender (*Lavandula angustifolia* 'Munstead') create a beautiful color combination. ❷ **'Kudos Mandarin' hummingbird mint** (*Agastache* 'Kudos Mandarin') is one of the hardiest orange-flowered cultivars available and is a beacon in the garden. ❸ **'Millenium' ornamental onion** (*Allium* 'Millenium') is a compact grower with excellent dark green foliage and rose flowers up to 24 inches tall. ❹ **'Northwind' switch grass** (*Panicum virgatum* 'Northwind') stands like a sentinel in the garden, and the frothy flowers stay tucked in the foliage rather than above it like most other cultivars. ❺ More than 200 tons of pink-hued quartzite gravel from South Dakota was spread 4 to 6 inches deep across the 1-acre site. Knowing it would be no small feat navigating all of the terraces, a boom truck was used to distribute the gravel. ❻ **'Blue Fortune' giant hyssop** (*Agastache* 'Blue Fortune') is one of the longest-blooming perennials in the gravel garden and attracts a multitude of butterflies from summer to fall. Its minty-scented foliage is deer-resistant. ❼ A clever "plant" sculpture is nestled into the plantings. ❽ **'Big Ears' lamb's ears** (*Stachys byzantina* 'Big Ears') is a tried-and-true, drought-tolerant plant that never fails to delight. ❾ **'Color Guard' Adam's needle** (*Yucca filamentosa* 'Color Guard') is among the most brilliantly colored and durable foliaged plants in the garden and looks great in every season.

Tall statured and cascading species help soften the stone walls during the growing season. The garden's composition is a blend of shrubs, vines, and perennials that add color in both flowers and foliage through the seasons. Together with diverse textures, their varied shapes--mounded, vertical, draping--bring structure and visual richness to the gravel garden.

A large space calls for large-scale plants to make an impact. Try plants like joe-pye weed (*Eutrochium maculatum*) (top), 'Ginger Love' fountain grass (*Pennisetum alopecuroides* 'Ginger Love') (right), 'Northwind' switch grass (*Panicum virgatum* 'Northwind') (far right), Hubricht's bluestar (*Amsonia hubrichtii*) next to Kara (opposite top left), and Russian sage (*Perovskia atriplicifolia*) (opposite bottom). The bold design of Ed Lyon (opposite, top right) continues to wow visitors to Reiman Gardens.

In 2019, the Hillside Water-wise Garden was one of twenty-one gardens featured in the U.S. Botanic Garden's exhibit "Celebrating New American Gardens" in Washington, D.C. Today, the terraced garden is the perfect backdrop for two annual events including Spirits in the Garden with hundreds of carved jack-o'-lanterns displayed along the garden's walls, and Winter Wonderscape with a holiday light show projected on the garden's facade. Learn more at www.reimangardens.com.

STEPHEN F. AUSTIN STATE UNIVERSITY
Nacogdoches, Texas

Living Laboratory in the Deep South

Award-winning horticulture professor Jared Barnes is always looking for new ideas to spark wonder among his students at Stephen F. Austin State University (SFASU) in Nacogdoches, Texas. At Plantery, their classroom botanical garden, Jared and his students trial native plants, experiment with propagation techniques in greenhouses, try new vegetable plants in a micro farm, and design a matrix-style food prairie for insects. Now, they're creating a gravel garden.

"I'd been following early pioneers in gravel gardening and was curious about growing plants and minimizing weeds in these stressful environments, so I thought it would be a great concept to introduce to students, especially here in the Deep South where weeds thrive year-round," says Jared. "We're always trying to teach them different ways to do things."

As he introduced gravel gardens to his students, he talked about the weed challenges in the Southeast during the active growing season as well as the mild yet cooler months when winter weeds continue to grow. The students expressed their own frustrations in managing weeds while waiting for Plantery's new naturalistic plantings to fill in and choke out weeds. Here, they often resorted to mulch, preemergent herbicides, and plenty of hand-weeding and cultivating to manage weeds.

Jared explained to them the science of weed management and how an inorganic mulch, like gravel, can increase the stress of site conditions and lower the level of nitrogen in the soil. Even with all this knowledge, he and his students had their doubts.

He challenged them: "Would common perennials grow in gravel here in the Deep South with our extreme summer temperatures and prolonged droughts?" Fortunately, the students responded enthusiastically.

They assembled a list of plants to both order and propagate. To get started, they chose switch grass, salvia, aster, calamint, feather grass, and mountain mint. Students created designs for the 400-square-foot, quarter-circle space. Jared then synthesized the designs together with taller plants along the back edge, a curving pathway through the middle, and an arrangement of anchor and satellite plants along each side. They also incorporated some larger existing rocks as part of the design.

The gravel garden was installed in April 2021. Jared led the students as they prepped the site, leveled the soil, enclosed the space with a rock border, and filled it with 6 cubic yards of gravel. Jared sourced blue-gray, baked-clay gravel from a local source. To keep the gravel depth even, students inserted stakes with two markings—one for the soil line and one 4 inches higher for the gravel line.

With the gravel layer complete, students added the plants following Jared's instructions. He advised them to dig a hole in the gravel, pull the plant from the container, remove some soil from its root ball, toss the excess soil in tubs, place the plant

OPPOSITE From left to right: SFASU students Amiah, Sydney, and Tess were eager to try a gravel garden and wondered if plants would thrive in gravel in the Deep South with its hot summers and long droughts. They were delighted to see not only the plants flourish, but the weeds disappear.

plantery
STEPHEN F. AUSTIN STATE UNIVERSITY

Students designed and installed this 400-square-foot corner garden with taller plants like muhly grasses along the back edge, a curving pathway through the middle, and an arrangement of anchor and satellite plants like asters along each side. They also added a rock edge and larger accent rocks.

in the hole, then cover with gravel. Once planted, the students thoroughly watered the plants.

After the planting was complete, Jared and his students still wondered if the plants would survive. One horticulture student shared that he showed the new planting to his parents, owners of a garden nursery, and they too expressed their doubts.

"I'll be honest with you, I don't know either," he told his student. "If everything fails, we can just take the gravel up and use it for a patio or path."

By fall, the prototype garden flourished. All but the switch grass and joe-pye weed thrived, and the gravel layer effectively held back the weeds.

"We're in Texas, where weeds grow fast, so I was impressed with how the gravel layer held them back," says Jared.

To further enhance the garden's beauty and seasonal interest, the students added spring-flowering bulbs like daffodils and grape hyacinths. They also experimented with penstemons and bluebonnets, hoping these self-sowers would reseed in the gravel. They had to thin coneflowers, welcomed tall verbenas that appeared serendipitously, and fertilized asters that needed more nutrients.

Jared reports maintenance is minimal. In late winter, he and the students cut back the plant material, add it to a compost pile, and blow away any remaining organic matter.

For those considering a gravel garden in the South, Jared offers valuable advice. He recommends using larger, quart-size plants since smaller plugs will dry out too quickly. Frequent watering is essential during the initial establishment period, roughly every other day for six to eight weeks. Spring is the ideal planting time to take advantage of cooler temperatures and spring rains.

There are concerns about gravel gardens getting hot in the Deep South. But as long as the plant foliage knits together, the gravel getting too hot isn't much of a problem.

Encouraged by the success of the initial gravel garden, Jared plans to create a series of similar gravel gardens to trial a variety of native plants.

"I think we'll find many of the native species are well suited to growing in gravel and will show less flop and disease compared to plants grown in fertile soil," he says.

ABOVE Jared and his students are always trialing plants to find those that can not only survive but also thrive. Extremes in temperature and moisture have always been the norm in southeast Texas, but now like in other parts of the world, climate change is making it even more unpredictable and extreme. Jared and other experts believe that their current local climate conditions will be very similar to what others in the northern parts of the United States will experience in future years. OPPOSITE Award-winning horticulture professor Jared Barnes is always looking for new ideas to spark wonder among his students. "I'd been following early pioneers in gravel gardening and was curious about growing plants and minimizing weeds in these stressful environments, so I thought it would be a great concept to introduce to students, especially here in the Deep South where weeds thrive year-round," he says.

Plant Survival Strategies

Plants can't move out of the way of danger, so they have evolved traits to help them survive environmental stresses and disturbances. Stresses include drought, cold, and flooding while disturbances include fire, animal browse, and wind.

Plant Categories

Ecologist J. Philip Grime researched these plant survival strategies and classified them in three broad categories:

1) **COMPETITORS** rule when stress and disturbance are low; they grow tall like joe-pye weed or wide like rough goldenrod and beebalm.

2) **STRESS TOLERATORS** take tough growing conditions in stride; their growth rate is slow and they take time to grow from seed, like Adam's needle, false indigo, and prairie dropseed.

3) **RUDERALS** pop up when the odds are favorable for growth; these short-lived plants like California poppy, columbine and Texas bluebonnet produce copious amounts of seed to ensure their annual return in unstable environments.

Survival Strategies to Promote Plant Diversity

Starting with gravel gardens, Jared offers these strategies to create an environment that welcomes a broader plant palette.

- Plant in a 4- to 6-inch layer of gravel or sand to hold back weeds and create infertile conditions for stress-tolerating plants.
- Water and fertilize less. It not only conserves resources and saves money but diversifies your plant palette.
- Disturb plants by breaking up the edges of competitors to allow room for ruderals to pop up.
- Cut back vigorous growers like asters and catmints in spring to keep their growth in check.

ABOVE As students installed plants, they learned how some plants can adapt to environmental stresses like drought, and disturbances like wind.

A blue-gray, baked-clay gravel (top left) was sourced locally and spread in a 4-inch layer. Coneflowers (top right) were prolific and even had to be thinned. Prairie dropseed (bottom left) and aromatic aster (bottom right) thrived in the gravel layer.

❶ **Mexican feather grass** (*Nassella tenuissima*) is a Texas native and well-adapted to the fluctuations in weather. ❷ **Rattlesnake master** (*Eryngium yuccifolium*) would be considered a ruderal—a short-lived plant that pops up when conditions are favorable and produces lots of seed to ensure its return in the future. ❸ **Rose verbena** (*Glandularia canadensis*) is native in the eastern half of the United States and was previously in the genus *Verbena*. It is a very drought-tolerant species that often reseeds in the gravel garden. A gulf fritillary sips nectar from the tiny flowers. ❹ **Pale purple coneflower** (*Echinacea pallida*) seed heads are left standing for birds to feed on.

ABOVE Castor bean (*Ricinus communis*) initially seeded into the gravel garden from a nearby annual bed and now does every year without fail. The students like the exotic feel it adds to the garden; they weed out most as they are just emerging but always leave a few for fun. **ABOVE LEFT AND LEFT** To add some ornamentation and a consistent supply of nectar for pollinators, drought-tolerant annuals can be added to the gravel garden. An eastern carpenter bee finds nourishment on an annual salvia, and zinnias add a punch of color.

WELCOME!
We are the Plantery, a student botanic garden rooted within SFA's Department of Agriculture.
We cultivate passionate students who grow and celebrate incredible plants that elevate and inspire our community.
Come grow with us! Use the QR code to learn about events, volunteer opportunities, and more!
plantery

At Plantery, their fun and educational classroom botanical garden is all about hands-on learning. Jared and his students trial native plants, experiment with propagation and growing techniques in greenhouses, try new vegetable plants in a micro farm, and design a matrix-style food prairie for insects. Now, they're also caring for the gravel garden they created.

Plantery

In winter, Amiah and Sydney cut back the plant material, add it to a compost pile, blow away any remaining organic matter, and refresh a little gravel where needed. Learn more about SFASU Gardens at www.sfasu.edu/academics/colleges/forestry-agriculture/research-outreach/sfa-gardens.

Gravel in British Public Gardens

BETH CHATTO GARDENS

Essex, England

Car Park to Paradise

In 1990, renowned British horticulturist Beth Chatto faced a curious challenge: transforming a ¾-acre former parking lot with heavily compacted soil into a thriving garden. She envisioned a garden of decorative plants that could thrive, undeterred by the region's low rainfall and desiccating winds, without supplemental water under the harsh conditions of southeast England. Three decades later, this iconic gravel garden epitomizes her pioneering gardening spirit, carries on her lifelong dedication to plant ecology, and inspires countless visitors.

"Beth and her husband, Andrew, were very much about 'right plant and right place' and working with nature versus against it," says Julia Boulton, Beth's granddaughter and the garden's chairman.

The garden started when Beth decided to move a car park (parking lot) and was left with a vacant lot. Its naturally sandy, gravelly soil and full sun presented the perfect spot to create a garden reminiscent of a dry riverbed she spotted years prior on a trip to New Zealand with another British garden legend Christopher Lloyd. The challenge was to adapt this concept to Essex, one of England's driest regions, and do so without irrigation.

Beth's expert choice of plants was crucial to the garden's success. She selected drought-tolerant species, many native to Mediterranean climates. Beth credits her husband's extensive knowledge of plants and their native habitats as a significant influence on her approach.

In her book, *Beth Chatto's Gravel Garden*, she details the eight-year journey of what she calls "a horticulture experiment." The project began in the fall of 1991, with a subsoiler turning the heavily compacted soil 2 feet deep. A borrowed farm roller was used to flatten the soil lightly, then Beth laid out the initial design using garden hoses. Her informal pattern included deep side borders, six island beds, and a sinuous path mimicking the dried-up riverbed.

Beth and her team amended the soil with homemade compost to provide initial nourishment for the new plants. From there, she drew up plant lists.

"She was inspired by *ikebana*," says Julia about the Japanese art of flower arranging. "She planted tall upright vertical plants to lead the eyes to the sky, added a middle layer, then low ground covers."

Once the soil settled in early spring, Beth covered the paths with gravel and began planting. She dunked the potted plants in water to saturate their root balls before placing them in the garden. For the first year, her gardeners diligently hoed out any seedlings to prevent weeds. The next spring, the beds were mulched with a 2-inch layer of gravel.

The garden faced its first major test during two summers of drought with unusually high temperatures and minimal rainfall. The soil beneath the gravel mulch dried out, causing plants to show signs of stress. While Beth was tempted to reach for the garden hose, nursery manager David Ward urged her to stick to the experiment and observe the plants' resilience without supplemental water. Her perseverance paid off as cooler weather and rain revived the plants, leading to fresh growth.

Early encouragement came as she was planning her experiment when she visited filmmaker and artist Derek Jarman's gravel garden project in the

OPPOSITE In 1990, renowned British horticulturist Beth Chatto transformed a 3/4-acre former parking lot with heavily compacted soil into a thriving garden. Three decades later, this iconic gravel garden epitomizes her pioneering gardening spirit, carries on her lifelong dedication to plant ecology, and inspires countless visitors.

The former parking lot's naturally sandy, gravelly soil and full sun presented the perfect spot to create a dried riverbed she'd admired from her travels. Using garden hoses, she laid out deep side borders, six island beds, and a sinuous path mimicking the riverbed.

coastal town of Dungeness, 67 miles to her south (see the next chapter). In her book, she retells the chance encounter with Derek as she and Christopher were exploring a beach nearby and accidentally came upon Derek's beach gravel garden. As she learned of Derek's AIDS diagnosis and the emotional healing power of crafting this creative space, she left inspired to continue her work despite the challenges she faced in creating the new garden. Beth left feeling reassured having seen him successfully use a palette of plants similar to what she had in mind for her own garden.

"There will be disappointments and failures," Beth wrote, "but every day I feel a sense of wonder and delight at what plants can do if given a chance."

Over the decades, the garden has evolved, retaining only those plants truly suited to drought conditions. Since its inception, the garden has never been watered, apart from times of rejuvenating or replanting an area, and it informs a new generation with its sustainability, biodiversity, and beauty.

"The garden is evolving, yet it still very much feels like her garden," says Åsa Gregers-Warg, head gardener who joined in 2001. For example, while yarrow was part of the initial planting, it struggled with the harsh conditions and was replaced with more resilient later additions such as silver feather grass, 'Red Cauli' sedum, and California native Coulter's Matilija poppy.

"Everybody loves the gravel garden," says Julia and notes that while they think it's low-maintenance with its tough, hardy plants, it requires meticulous care due to its thin gravel layer. "With the way it is planted, you have to have experienced gardeners who know how to spot weeds and thin annuals with a crystal ball to the future," she says.

Beth's work ethic and attention to detail have left a lasting impact. Åsa recalls Beth as a driven, focused individual with a deep understanding of plants. "She was a hard taskmaster, and she taught me how to appreciate plant texture, shape, and form."

Since Beth's passing in 2018 at the age of ninety-four, her legacy continues through the Beth Chatto Education Trust, established in 2015. Julia now leads the organization dedicated to promoting Beth's "right plant, right place" philosophy. Through the continued dedication of her team, Beth's legacy lives on. Her gravel garden remains a beacon of sustainable, low-water gardening—a message that is more important now than ever.

"Beth inspired me with her energy, her teaching, and dedication to getting her message out," says Julia. "I have a responsibility to pass on that valuable message of sustainability."

ABOVE Beth, known for her work ethic and attention to detail, has left a lasting impact. "She was inspired by *ikebana*," says Julia. "She planted tall, upright vertical plants to lead the eyes to the sky, added a middle layer, then low ground covers." OPPOSITE Gravel gardening pioneer Beth Chatto is one of the foremost modern gardeners and a holder of the Royal Horticultural Society's Victoria Medal of Honour. Her gardening books include the classics *Beth Chatto's Green Tapestry*, *The Dry Garden*, and *The Damp Garden*.

"Beth inspired me with her energy, her teaching and dedication to getting her message out. I have a responsibility to pass on that valuable message of sustainability," says Julia Boulton, Beth's granddaughter and the garden's chairman, shown here (left) with head gardener Åsa Gregers-Warg (right).

“The garden is evolving, yet it still very much feels like her garden,” says Åsa. For example, while yarrow was part of the initial planting, it struggled with the harsh conditions and was replaced with more resilient later additions such as silver feather grass, ‘Red Cauli’ sedum, and California native Coulter’s Matilija poppy. Learn more at www.bethchatto.co.uk.

Continuing Chatto's Mission in the Community

The first project, Chattowood, was initiated in 2022 when developers of a new eighty-home neighborhood approached Julia. They requested to name the development in honor of Beth and Andrew Chatto. Julia agreed and in return asked if the Beth Chatto team could be involved in the design and planting of the site, so it reflected the garden's ethos. The developers graciously accepted, and the team welcomed the opportunity to introduce sustainable gravel gardening techniques as an alternative to conventional lawns and landscaped beds that dominate so many developments.

Still, this project was unlike the intricate and high-maintenance gravel garden at Beth Chatto Gardens. These Chattowood gardens were designed with an 11-inch layer of locally sourced sand and gravel and featured tough plants that are not prolific self-seeders. The thick sand layer, which forms a hard surface crust, was intended to greatly reduce weed seeds from germinating and encourage the plants to develop a deep root system, making them more resilient to drought. The project proved a success, with gardens thriving despite an unexpected ten-week drought. The borders were watered with a hosepipe (to limit the amount of water used) during the heatwave, something they wouldn't normally do. The plantings now delight residents and attract a diverse range of wildlife from hummingbird hawk moths to bees and butterflies.

The second project was Colchester's Meanwhile Garden, which opened in July 2024. This initiative transformed a long-abandoned brownfield site into a vibrant public pocket park. The project, suggested by a local county councilor, involved recycling rubble from a former bus station to create a planting medium. Beth Chatto's team partnered with urban garden designer Darryl Moore to design the garden that featured both ornamental and spontaneous wild plants to support a rich insect population. Grown and planted by the Beth Chatto team, the plant palette included Russian sage, giant mullein, vervain, wild carrot, wormwood, and yarrow.

"These plants are tough and resilient—perfect for an empty lot," says Julia. "You don't need to be looking after them all the time."

The garden's maintenance relies on volunteers and ongoing advice from Beth Chatto's horticulturists. The plants have thrived in the transformed site, demonstrating the effectiveness of the Chatto gravel gardening principles.

Two recent projects extend the legacy of Beth Chatto's Gardens to the surrounding community, including Chattowood, a new neighborhood adjacent to the gardens, and the Meanwhile Garden on a former brownfield in Colchester. Learn more about Chattowood at www.bethchatto.co.uk/projects/chattowood.htm

PROSPECT COTTAGE
Dungeness, England

Beacon of Creativity and Hope

Along a gravelly beach at Prospect Cottage, driftwood totems rise among subdued patches of gorse and sea kale during the winter months at this surreal oasis near the Dungeness power plant in southern England. Come spring, the tar-black fishing cottage bursts into life with a riot of colorful blooms, including golden poppies, blue cornflowers, and pink penstemons. This iconic cottage garden—a beacon of creativity and hope—was the brainchild of avant-garde filmmaker, writer, artist, and AIDS activist Derek Jarman, who began cultivating it in the 1990s. Derek's bold, defiant style during his final years with AIDS left a lasting impression, continuing to inspire through the efforts of its subsequent caretakers: first, Derek's partner Keith Collins, and more recently, head gardener Jonny Bruce.

Derek purchased Prospect Cottage at age 44 following his HIV diagnosis. He soon started gardening its half-acre plot along the gravel beach (or "shingle" as it's called in the United Kingdom). He chronicled his experiences in books *Modern Nature* and *Derek Jarman's Garden*. He described gathering large flint stones and driftwood and arranging them in mystical circles. He even used one piece of driftwood to mark a wild rose he discovered. A passionate gardener from childhood, he was inspired by that wild rose and planted more roses reminiscent of his family's English garden.

Derek soon realized Dungeness's leaf-scorching, salt-laden winds and thick shoreline of pure gravel made it difficult for lush cottage garden plants to thrive. Instead, he turned to deep-rooted, drought-tolerant native plants—sea kale, valerian, viper's bugloss, and teasels. He dug trenches in the gravel and filled them with amended soil. He covered the underground pockets with pebbles to make them appear as though plants were miraculously growing from the pebbles. He often used driftwood sticks to mark out new plants and pockets sown with annual seeds. He would adorn the sticks with found objects—crab shells, chains, and twisted wire—from his daily beach walks.

"You see it is rather a wild garden," wrote Derek, advocating for the use of native plants over manicured lawns. He encouraged readers to embrace the wildness, claiming, "it will bring you much happiness."

In front, he arranged circles of shrubby evergreen gorse alongside drought-tolerant, exotic plants like dianthus, santolina, and African daisies that he found at nearby nurseries. In back, he designed a "random" garden interspersing plants among more driftwood and found objects like anchors and rusted metal engine parts. One of his later, short-lived projects involved building raised beds for vegetables.

Over the years, Derek forged connections with garden legend Beth Chatto and exchanged garden visits with renowned gardener Christopher Lloyd.

In a television interview with producer Jeremy Isaacs toward the end of his life, Derek shared: "Every flower is a triumph. I've had more fun from this place than I've had with anything else in my life. I should have always been a gardener."

After Derek's death in 1994, his partner Keith inherited Prospect Cottage. The two shared a deep bond, meeting in 1987 at a screening of one of Derek's films. They divided their time between

OPPOSITE This iconic cottage garden along the beach or "shingle" of southern England was the brainchild of avant-garde film producer, writer, artist, and AIDS activist Derek Jarman, who began cultivating it in the 1990s. Derek's bold, defiant style during his final years with AIDS left a lasting impression and continues to inspire.

PROSPECT COTTAGE

Located near the Dungeness power plant, this surreal oasis bursts into life with a riot of colorful spring blooms, including rich golden poppies, cheerful ox-eye daisies, deep pink penstemons, and magenta- and white-flowered valerians.

London—where Keith appeared in three of Derek's films—and the cottage. Following Derek's passing, Keith took on the role of steward, managing the property with limited resources while working as a fisherman and later a driver on the London Underground.

When Keith was diagnosed with a terminal brain tumor, it was his hope that the cottage could be preserved for the future. A campaign by Art Fund raised £3.6 million to purchase it and fund a permanent public program, the conservation and maintenance of the building, its collection, its contents, and its renowned garden—all of which are now managed by Creative Folkestone with support from Tate and the Art Fund.

Keith enlisted head gardener Jonny Bruce, who had first visited Prospect Cottage in 2012 while studying art history at Cambridge and was profoundly influenced by Derek's writings.

Jonny credits his mother for introducing him to the garden; when he was struggling with his academic direction, she gifted him a copy of *Modern Nature*, which challenged his previously dismissive view of gardens as mere "window dressings." This new thought led him to write his thesis on Prospect Cottage and pursue gardening as a career.

"It was this revelation that gardens could be so much more than what I thought and opened my eyes to the potential of gardens as places of creative expression," says Jonny. "It was really exciting reading this book where Derek fused his queer rage with this most beautifully poetic prose through the lens of a garden."

After graduating in 2013, Jonny undertook a garden apprenticeship in Wales, followed by a two-year scholarship at the legendary garden of the late Christopher Lloyd, Great Dixter in Northiam, just 20 miles west of Dungeness. While at Dixter, he reached out to Keith to see if he could help in the garden. Keith welcomed Jonny's offer and after a couple visits, mailed him the keys to tend the garden even while he was away.

"Keith was quite guarded," recalls Jonny, "but once you had his trust, he was incredibly generous."

Feeling the weight of Derek's legacy, Jonny was initially apprehensive about altering the garden and fretted over "every blade of grass preordained by Derek." However, as he worked alongside Keith, he gained confidence and learned to embrace a more dynamic approach to the garden as an evolving art form. "There's this danger that people don't feel empowered to engage with these cult personalities in gardening and art because they're too precious about the original intention," he notes.

Keith viewed his role as a steward rather than an owner, a perspective that provided Jonny with a valuable framework for his approach. Today, Jonny plays this role primarily by editing the ever-changing garden. He attempts to maintain the aesthetic Derek established, influenced partly by experiences of Zen gardens on trips to Japan with Keith.

"The garden is a shifting tapestry of predominantly self-sown plants, so you're going in and removing plants to control the balance," he explains.

Jonny recognizes the shingle has evolved—from pure gravel to the grassy lot Derek first found, to its current condition with planting pockets of amended soil throughout. And many plantings, especially the denser plantings near the house, have developed as plant material breaks down into organic matter over time. Rather than amend the shingle too much, Jonny has chosen to add tough plants that are better adapted to the natural Dungeness conditions.

He has embarked on new projects with the extra resources from Art Fund. In the ill-adapted vegetable beds, he replaced the soil with sand and planted one bed with a medicinal garden of tough Mediterranean herbs like rosemary, sage, and marjoram, while the other has been established with a trial garden of shrubby Turkish sages. Along the roadside, he also planted rockrose and lavender cotton to reduce the number of tourists from driving onto the shingle and getting stuck, an all-too-frequent occurrence.

"Derek had a real affinity for plants and would have enjoyed seeing the new plantings," says Jonny. He even found plant labels from Derek and was delighted to learn many were plants he was experimenting with in the updated gardens.

Fostering community engagement remains a priority for Jonny. He organizes volunteer weekends to maintain the garden's dynamic and living connection to its past.

"My role as the gardener isn't to stamp my signature on it; it's about being a steward like Keith and making gentle interventions to ensure the garden remains relevant," he explains.

Looking ahead, Jonny envisions passing on the stewardship of the garden to a new caretaker, ensuring Derek's garden legacy—through Keith and now himself—continues to flourish and inspire for generations to come.

Derek (inset) purchased Prospect Cottage at age forty-four following his HIV diagnosis. He soon started gardening its half-acre plot and chronicled his experiences in books *Modern Nature* and *Derek Jarman's Garden*. He described gathering large flint stones and driftwood and arranging them in mystical circles.

OPPOSITE Derek often used driftwood sticks to mark out new plants. He would adorn the sticks with found objects--crab shells, chains, and twisted wire--from his daily beach walks.

ABOVE Dungeness's leaf-scorching, salt-laden winds and thick shoreline of pure gravel made it difficult for lush cottage garden plants to thrive. Instead, Derek turned to deep-rooted, drought-tolerant native plants--sea kale, valerian, viper's bugloss, and teasel. **RIGHT** Derek dug trenches in the gravel and filled them with amended soil and plants or seeds like common foxglove (pictured here). He covered the underground pockets with pebbles to make it appear as though plants were miraculously growing from the pebbles.

OPPOSITE Throughout the garden, Derek planted herbs and a "pharmacopeia" of medicinal plants such as poppy, rosemary, sage, lavender, and marjoram. LEFT Derek interspersed plants, like these California poppies, among art and found objects like small boulders and metal engine parts. BELOW Shingle, shells, and found art intermingle.

RIGHT When Derek passed in 1994, his partner Keith Collins cared for the garden for 20 years, then passed the responsibilities to its current steward, Jonny Bruce (pictured here). Today, Jonny fulfills this role by editing the ever-changing garden. "The garden is a shifting tapestry of predominantly self-sown plants, so you're going in and removing plants to control the balance," he explains.

PROSPECT COTTAGE

"Derek had a real affinity for plants and would have enjoyed seeing the new plantings," says Jonny. He even found plant labels from Derek and was delighted to learn many were plants he was experimenting with in the new gardens. Learn more at www.creativefolkestone.org.uk/prospect-cottage.

SISSINGHURST CASTLE GARDEN
Kent, England

Delos Revival

If Vita Sackville-West and Harold Nicolson were alive today, they would be thrilled to see the recent transformation of the Delos Garden at Sissinghurst Castle. Embracing the couple's same experimental spirit, the horticulture team has overcome soil and light challenges to breathe new life into this historically significant garden. This renovation not only honors Vita and Harold's legacy but also adopts a progressive approach to resilient garden design in the face of climate change.

In the 1930s, writer Vita and her husband, diplomat Harold, traveled to the ancient Greek island of Delos. Inspired by the island's natural beauty and romantic ruins, they returned to England with the ambitious goal of creating a Mediterranean garden among the other themed garden rooms at Sissinghurst. They constructed terraces, used rubble from the medieval mansion to create faux ruins, and introduced Mediterranean plants to evoke the feel of a rocky Greek hillside.

Unfortunately, the original Delos Garden never quite succeeded. The sun-loving species native to gravelly, well-drained soils struggled in the heavy clay and shade along the north-facing side of the Priest House. World War II further impacted the garden's care as garden crew left to serve. Despite the couple's intentions, the Delos Garden never achieved the vision they had imagined. By 1953 Vita wrote: "This has not been a success so far, but perhaps someday it will come right."

Fast-forward to 2016, when head gardener Troy Scott Smith recognized the potential for rejuvenating the Delos Garden as part of his overall effort to bring back the garden's history and its romantic style. He sought the expertise of landscape architect Dan Pearson, inviting him to serve as "godparent" to the garden. His role involved seasonal visits to provide an outside perspective and to workshop ideas together with Troy.

During one of their garden walks, they paused at the Delos corner that had evolved into a sleepy woodland garden. Here, Troy shared his aspirations for transforming the area into a modern interpretation of Vita and Harold's vision. With Dan's encouragement, Troy arranged for two Sissinghurst gardeners to visit Greece to immerse themselves in the landscape of Delos and beyond. This field trip would be key to informing the design process and enabling them to find inspiration in a way similar to Vita and Harold's experience.

Troy then commissioned Dan to design a plan to reimagine Delos through the eyes of Vita and Harold. Dan delved into the gardeners' field trip report and the Sissinghurst archives, which included a photo album of the couple's Greek cruise and early images of the garden.

"It was a very interesting thing to be doing then because in British gardens not many people were trying to reimagine a place," Dan said in a presentation to the Mediterranean Garden Society. He explained contemporary garden designers like William Robinson and Gertrude Jekyll were making naturalistic gardens but not taking them as wild, nor were they emulating specific places.

As he further reviewed the field trip notes and reflected on his own travels to Greece, he tried to

OPPOSITE In 2019, the horticulture team at Sissinghurst Castle reimagined Vita Sackville-West and Harold Nicolson's Delos Garden, originally created in the 1930s after a Mediterranean trip. Today, the garden not only embraces the Greek island's natural beauty and romantic ruins but also a progressive approach to resilient garden design.

Head gardener Troy Scott Smith called on landscape architect Dan Pearson to create a design that brings back the garden's history and romantic style. Drawing on the archives and the team's field trip notes to Delos, Dan envisioned a modern interpretation of Vita and Harold's vision with formal walled terraces along a central path and more rugged walled terraces meandering along intimate goat paths.

envision how Vita and Harold might have been charmed by the ephemeral floral displays and the juxtaposition of ruins overtaken by nature. He and his team visited Sissinghurst to survey the ¼-acre space. They observed the light challenges of the north-facing site and its large wall, the topography, significant trees, and the original well.

Dan came to envision a revitalized Delos Garden that evoked the rugged beauty of a Greek hillside, with walled terraced gardens that would capture both the essence of the original design and offer practical solutions for the soil and light challenges. His comprehensive plan included formal walled terraces along a central path with more rugged walled terraces meandering along intimate goat paths. Special moments featured upright stone columns and a boulder seating area around the original well.

For the plant design, Dan consulted with Olivier Filippi, a dry gardening expert who owned a Mediterranean plant nursery in southern France. Together, they compiled a list of Greek natives and plants from the wider Mediterranean region that could withstand the fluctuating weather conditions in the United Kingdom.

"The plants needed to be not just drought-tolerant but resilient to cope with downpours of rain; wet, cold winters; and long droughts in summer," says Saffron Prentis, Sissinghurst's assistant head gardener who led the Delos project.

She explains that Dan designed the plantings by zones, with 70 percent to be the phrygana zone (Mediterranean scrubland), which would include an all-silver zone, a scented zone along the goat paths, boundary zones with rough hedging, and shade zones along the walls and beneath the trees.

In 2019, Nigel Froggatt was engaged to begin construction with removal of 15 inches of clay and careful excavation around a few key trees, including an original kermes oak. They graded the land to form a series of terraced shelves. They laid perforated drainage pipe, then covered the area with a 10-inch layer of marine shingle—pebbles sourced from the United Kingdom's coastal regions. They brought in large, foundational boulders, then built the terrace walls around them.

For the terrace walls, they sourced Kentish ragstone—a hard, gray limestone native to the area. They built the walls using dry-laid techniques and tilted them southward to capture the sunlight. The wall designs featured two styles: formal cut stone for "city" walls along the main path and rugged boulders for more worn, "shepherd" walls along the goat paths.

"The idea was some of those rugged walls might look like they were knocked down by small goats," says Saffron.

To prepare terraces for planting, the team added French drains and a well-draining soil mix. Saffron says they experimented with various recipes. First, they started with a sandy soil recipe from nurseryman Olivier but found that British sand did not drain effectively. After further consultation, they created their own mix of locally sourced materials including ¼-inch ragstone gravel, crushed brick, and a low-nutrient topsoil used on British sugar beet farms. They then experimented with varying ratios of the three materials.

Saffron details how they filled a piece of pipe with the gravelly mix, then poured water into the pipe to see how the mix drained. They then followed with a second round of dousing to see how the water would drain through a saturated mix. After trialing different ratios, they refined the mix for the perfect balance: 50 percent gravel, 25 percent crushed brick, and 25 percent topsoil.

With the groundwork completed, plants were ordered from Olivier's nursery. He grew them in deep pots of various sizes—including 3-inch, 4-inch, and 1-quart—that allowed for long roots. In September 2019, just weeks before the COVID lockdown, the planting phase began. Dan joined the Sissinghurst horticulture team to place plants and give a master class in placement and planting strategies. To finish the space, they spread a 3- to 4-inch mulch layer of ragstone and strategically placed decorative elements, such as Harold's Grecian altars and tall columns from High Wall Garden in Oxford. The well head, a centerpiece of the garden, was renovated with a new stone cap.

After two challenging drought summers, the newly established garden thrived with no irrigation except for a few key trees. The gravel layer suppressed weeds, minimizing maintenance. The horticulture team edited overzealous plants and replaced failures like candelabrum sage (*Salvia interrupta*). They also cut back the garden at various stages throughout the season. Saffron explains the aim is for a looser style; she experimented with what she calls "goat pruning," as if Grecian goats were grazing the landscape. "We don't want anything to look too uniform because it is much more of a landscape than a garden," says Saffron. "There's a fine line between looking too gardened and tipping to where it's too woolly."

One of the most rewarding outcomes of the garden's transformation has been its increase in biodiversity. A recent biodiversity survey at Sissinghurst revealed that the Delos Garden was second only to the Orchard Meadow in supporting diverse wildlife.

"We've created a whole new habitat for creatures and insects," says Saffron.

Today, the team is introducing ephemerals into the garden. They're adding layers of spring bulbs and self-sowing annuals like poppies, nigella, and honeywort sown in pockets of sand and oyster shells.

Saffron emphasizes that the key to successfully managing a new gravel garden is to be patient with new plants. "Even when plants get knocked back by a bad winter, we wait and find things sprouting all of a sudden," she says. Other keys include learning to identify seedlings and editing out undesired plants to maintain the garden's balance. "There's an artistry in it," she says.

Looking to the future, plans are in motion to expand the garden. The removal of a 1980s garage will make room to extend the garden around the back of the Priest House and into a north garden.

As Vita once said, "The most noteworthy thing about gardeners is that they are always optimistic, always enterprising and never satisfied. They always look forward to doing something better than they have ever done before." This sentiment rings true in the bold reimagination of the Delos Garden today.

ABOVE For the terrace walls, they sourced Kentish ragstone--a hard, gray limestone native to the area. They built the walls using dry-laid techniques and tilted them southward to capture the sunlight.

Olivier Filippi, a dry gardening expert, advised on the planting design, compiling a list of Greek natives and plants from the wider Mediterranean region that could withstand the fluctuating weather conditions in the United Kingdom. Planting zones included an all-silver zone, a scented zone along the goat paths, boundary zones with rough hedging, and shade zones along the walls and beneath the trees.

Construction involved the removal of 15 inches of clay with careful excavation around a few key trees, including an original kermes oak. The land was graded to form a series of terraced shelves. They laid perforated drainage pipe, then covered the area with a 10-inch layer of marine shingle--pebbles sourced from the United Kingdom's coastal regions. They brought in large, foundational boulders, then built the terrace walls around them. The planting team, guided by Dan Pearson (above), installed plants in a tested mix of locally sourced materials including 5 percent ragstone gravel (1/4-inch), 25 percent crushed brick, and 25 percent low-nutrient topsoil used on British sugar beet farms.

OPPOSITE Assistant head gardener and Delos project leader, Saffron Prentis, stewards the select plantings in the garden. "The plants needed to be not just drought-tolerant but resilient to cope with downpours of rain; wet, cold winters; and long droughts in summer," says Saffron. Key plants include: Atlas mountain daisy (*Catananche caerulea* 'Tizi-n-Test'), Mediterranean wild thyme (*Thymbra capitata*), upright myrtle spurge (*Euphorbia rigida*), silky-spike melic grass (*Melica ciliata*), yarrow (*Achillea coarctata*), smokebush (*Cotinus coggygria*), partridge feather (*Tanacetum densum* ssp. *amani*), Grecian horehound (*Ballota pseudodictamnus*), Cretian pincushion flower (*Lomelosia cretica* or *Scabiosa cretica*), stonecrop (*Sedum sediforme*), annual honesty (*Lunaria annua* 'Corfu Blue'), and ornamental oregano (*Origanum laevigatum*).

Looking to the future, plans are in motion to expand the garden. The removal of a 1980s garage is underway and will make room to extend the garden around the back of the Priest House and into a north garden. Learn more at www.nationaltrust.org.uk/visit/kent/sissinghurst-castle-garden/recreating-delos-at-sissinghurst.

KNEPP CASTLE
West Sussex, England

Rewilded Walled Garden

Within the walled gardens of Knepp Castle, a vibrant tapestry of life unfolds. Dragonflies zip over tall grasses, beetles scuttle through gravel crevices, and the occasional elephant hawk moth flutters among the rich, naturalized plantings. This remarkable transformation—from an all-grass croquet lawn and traditional pool garden to a flourishing, biodiverse "rewilded" space—buzzes with activity. In just three years, the garden's invertebrate count has surged by an impressive 33 percent.

Head gardener Charlie Harpur attributes the garden's success to its plant complexity and selective herbivory approach to management. "We hope that the trajectory will continue to rise as the garden develops, and we make adjustments to add more pieces to our habitat mosaic," he says.

The garden's rewilding journey is part of a larger project that extends beyond its walls. Owner Charlie Burrell inherited the 3500-acre estate farm in 1987, and with his wife, Isabella Tree, author of *Wilding: The Return of Nature to a British Farm*, continued the family's centuries-old farming tradition for nearly two decades, but decided that something had to change. The ever-increasing costs of industrialized farming made it next to impossible for their farm to be profitable on the challenging soils at Knepp.

"Knepp is on 320 meters [1049 feet] of Wealden clay, which is very difficult to work, often flooded in the winter, then like cracked concrete in the summer," Harpur explained.

Frustrated by these difficulties, the couple began exploring alternative land-management approaches that were better suited to their land.

"After seeing a rewilding project in Holland, they decided to put their faith in nature," says Harpur. He explained they toured Oostvaardersplassen reserve in the Netherlands with ecologist Frans Vera and learned about its experiment in grazing ecology that was producing more diverse habitats for wildlife. This inspired them to explore similar land-management techniques for Knepp.

"They started taking out all the internal fences, about 250 miles of it—a staggering amount but quite indicative of how fragmented our farmland had become—and added a perimeter fence around the entire property made possible with government funding," he said. They introduced a variety of grazing animals including old English longhorn cattle, Tamworth pigs, and Exmoor ponies. "The longhorns are a primitive breed that's as close as you can get to the extinct aurochs—massive herbivores that roamed our landscapes in the Holocene," says Harpur. "The Tamworth pigs are the closest legal alternative to wild boar, and the Exmoor ponies are a tough, wild pony breed."

Each animal interacts with the landscape in different ways. "Some browse, some graze, and some disturb the soil with their hooves or rootling noses, for example" says Harpur.

Over 20 years later, "some amazing things have happened." The estate has seen a fabulous resurgence of species, including turtledoves, nightingales, and purple emperor butterflies.

Within their Victorian walled garden, the couple sought to apply similar principles on a smaller scale, hoping to inspire other gardeners throughout the United Kingdom. "Not everyone has 3500 acres

OPPOSITE Within the walled gardens of Knepp Castle, a vibrant tapestry of life unfolds. Dragonflies zip over tall grasses, beetles scuttle through gravel crevices, and the occasional elephant hawk moth flutters among the rich, naturalized plantings.

This remarkable transformation--from an all-grass croquet lawn and traditional pool garden to a flourishing, biodiverse, rewilded space--buzzes with activity. In just three years, the Rewilded Garden's invertebrate count has surged by an impressive 33 percent.

ABOVE

to rewild but an awful lot of people have gardens," Harpur notes. Charlie and Isabella assembled the garden project's advisory board, including landscape architect Tom Stuart-Smith who led the garden's design, botanist Mick Crawley, organic grower Jekka McVicar, and plant ecologist and designer James Hitchmough. Together, they asked the question: how do we rewild a garden?

They decided that humans could play the role of herbivores, roughing up the ground and pruning the plants in a graze-like manner. Harpur, who was working as a landscape architect at Stuart-Smith's studio, later joined the Knepp team. He says the rewilding of the pool garden began by excavating the flat croquet lawn and creating a 3D surface of "humps and hollows" to mimic a more natural landscape. They varied soil fertility and drainage by laying a patchwork of different planting media, including sand, soil, and even recycled crushed brick and concrete from a building project on the estate.

In November of 2021, more than 14,000 plants were carefully selected by Tom and James and planted to match the varying ecological conditions. The diverse palette includes species native to dry, stony riverbeds, mountain scree slopes, and rocky deserts around the world. "We planted native U.K. species alongside plants from farther south in Europe and other Mediterranean climates for an extra layer of resilience in our changing climate," says Harpur.

The garden was planted with a mix of small potted plants, bare-rooted grasses, and perennials. Accent plants, small trees, and woody shrubs were placed first, followed by clumps and drifts of other species. Finally, single plants were "dotted" throughout to mimic the random dispersal of seeds by the wind.

James, world-renowned for his meadow-making techniques, was responsible for the planting design on the 150-foot-long, north-south-running dry ridge, affectionately called "Hitchmough Ridge." His selected species of plants were strategically placed along the varying topography—plants from moist habitats at the base of a slope, others from hotter, drier habitats along the coarse ridge. A seed mix of 43 species of perennials was sown across the planted area. The seed was mixed with sawdust from Knepp's sawmill and distributed by the handful.

Despite challenging weather conditions, the garden has thrived, even establishing "a bit too well in places" with an abundance of spreading bellflower (*Campanula patula*) and nine beardtongues (including *Penstemon barbatus* 'Coccineus', *P. cobaea*, *P. ovatus*, and *P. grandiflorus*). Of the 43 species sown, only five have not yet emerged.

The Knepp garden team, including Harpur and four additional part-time gardeners, welcomes the garden's dynamism and unpredictability. They see their roles as similar to herbivores, so they prune as animals would have grazed, preventing particularly "happy" species from dominating the plantings. "People expect a rewilded garden to be hands-off," he said, "but the garden ecosystem relies on mimicking natural processes, so the gardeners serve as the herbivores." He explains this care requires a different mindset—thinking like a water buffalo, a pig, or a wild pony.

For example, when dealing with weeds, the team intervenes judiciously, grazing and pulling them, to support greater diversity. They've created a scoring system for weeds based on factors such as the number of invertebrate species they support, their ecological benefits (for example, breaking up clay with their taproots), their likelihood of reseeding or spreading aggressively, their difficulty eradicating if they get out of hand, and their visual appeal.

"Depending on their score, they might be on the grazing menu a little more or less often," says Harpur. Recently, annual fleabane (*Erigeron annuus*) and oxeye daisy (*Leucanthemum vulgare*)—though both popular with pollinators—were "grazed" a little more aggressively due to their potential to quickly dominate if not managed.

Pruning is also carried out in a selective manner. Instead of a single end-of-season cutback, the team grazes some plants to the ground while leaving seed heads on some and allowing others to decay.

"Nothing is done uniformly," says Harpur. "We try mixing it up as much as we can in order to have a more complex range of habitats and hopefully see more of an uplift in wildlife."

The garden is a true experiment, even surprising the team when the ponies accidentally got into the garden and grazed selectively instead of destroying all the plants. With the recent invertebrate survey demonstrating the positive impact of the garden's diversity, the team continues to refine its approach, creating more niches and planting more species to attract even more insects.

Now that the garden is thriving, the Knepp team is hosting workshops and garden safaris to share its findings with the gardening community. Their garden journey is also captured in their blog, while the broader Knepp rewilding story is covered in *Wilding*—of which a film has been made—and *The Book of Wilding* (a more practical guide). With about 23 million gardens in the United Kingdom, Harpur remains hopeful about the positive role each can play in mitigating climate change and restoring wildlife.

ABOVE Head gardener Charlie Harpur skillfully cares for Knepp's Rewilded Garden, which is a part of a larger rewilding journey that extends well beyond its boundaries. The walled garden is a more practical example of the rewilding initiative for fellow gardeners. "Not everyone has 3500 acres to rewild but an awful lot of people have gardens," Harpur notes.

Just because a garden is designed and managed in a more naturalistic manner doesn't mean it can't be beautiful. Vibrant, artful combinations of native and non-native plants support a myriad of insects and other creatures. With the recent invertebrate survey demonstrating the positive impact of the garden's diversity, the team continues to refine its approach, creating more niches and planting additional species to attract even more life.

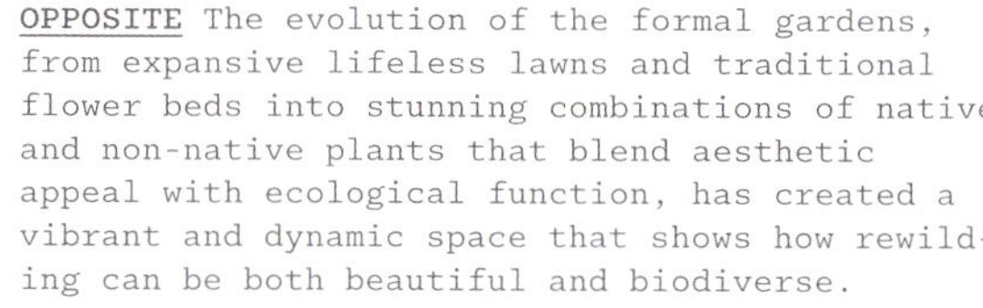

OPPOSITE The evolution of the formal gardens, from expansive lifeless lawns and traditional flower beds into stunning combinations of native and non-native plants that blend aesthetic appeal with ecological function, has created a vibrant and dynamic space that shows how rewilding can be both beautiful and biodiverse.

In November of 2021, more than 14,000 plants were carefully selected to match the varying ecological conditions. The garden was planted with a mix of small potted plants, bare-rooted grasses, and perennials. “We planted native U.K. species alongside plants from farther south in Europe and other Mediterranean climates for an extra layer of resilience in our changing climate,” says Harpur.

"People expect a rewilded garden to be hands-off," says Charlie Harpur, head gardener, "but the garden ecosystem relies on mimicking natural processes, so the gardeners serve as the herbivores." He and four other part-time gardeners judiciously prune plants and pull weeds to support greater diversity, mimicking what native animals would have done through grazing and foraging for food in the wild.

In contrast to the former traditional gardens, the varied and dynamic plantings change through the seasons, offering beauty for visitors while also providing food and habitat for wildlife. Faded flowers are left to supply seed for birds and small mammals, and the standing stems throughout fall and winter serve as refuge for insect eggs and larvae that will awaken in spring. The tranquil, muted tones and unique forms and shapes of the dormant garden's foliage and seed structures are just as captivating as the brilliant flowers of spring and summer.

The Rewilded Garden is part of a larger grazing ecology experiment that extends beyond its walls to the 3500-acre estate farm. Here, herds of grazing animals wander the former farm fields, reshaping the land and creating new habitats for wildlife. Over twenty years later, the estate has seen a fabulous resurgence of species, including turtledoves, nightingales, and purple emperor butterflies. Learn more at www.knepp.co.uk/knepp-estate/gardens/rewild-a-garden.

Gravel at Work

EPIC HEADQUARTERS
Verona, Wisconsin

Massive Rooftop Solution

When envisioning landscape plantings for an expansive rooftop garden at software company Epic's headquarters, Jeff Epping found inspiration in the idea of a gravel garden. Having previously experimented with smaller-scale gravel gardens on the company's first campus in 2007, Jeff saw an opportunity to elevate the concept to "epic" proportions on this 3-acre rooftop.

"The roof of this underground parking garage had shallow soil and weight restrictions, so it ruled out tree plantings and water-thirsty plants," says Jeff, whose expertise has guided Epic's landscaping endeavors for more than 20 years. "A gravel garden seemed like the perfect solution."

At the time, gravel gardens were a relatively novel concept, with other naturalistic garden styles like meadows and matrix plantings yet to gain widespread recognition. From the start, the design team tried to stay away from large expanses of lawn, typical of corporate landscapes, so they designed large mixed border plantings with lots of shrubs and complementary perennials. The beds and borders were definitely more eco-friendly than turf, but they did require a good bit of labor to maintain, including edging, mulching, deadheading, and weeding. Continuing this style on the new rooftop would be a challenge, especially since conventional trucks are too heavy to transport mulch onto the site.

Jackie Hager, Epic's long-tenured horticulturist, acknowledges the daunting project: "When you're talking about 3 acres, it's going to be a lot of work well into the future—not just on the front-end installing plantings, but a ton of ongoing maintenance." The allure of reduced maintenance made gravel gardens an appealing choice despite their untested nature in such a large space—and on a roof to boot.

"Heck if we can reduce the maintenance and create beautiful gardens, it will be a win for the future," Jackie recalls Jeff telling the design team.

Concerns persisted about weed suppression and plant survival in the exposed, heat-radiating environment of the gravel-filled rooftop. The garden's performance was critical, with its central location among five buildings.

"No one had done a green roof gravel garden on this scale before," she says.

Yet Jeff, Jackie, and the horticulture team saw potential in the innovative approach. Presenting the concept to Epic's founder and CEO, Judy Faulkner, proved pivotal. She embraced the eco-friendly garden and how it aligned with Epic's commitment to sustainability and creativity, showcased at its intelligently designed corporate headquarters. The campus features cleverly themed buildings, including a farm-themed campus complete with barn, shed, and stable.

With Judy's support, the project began in 2010. Landscape architect Linda Sievert fleshed out the gravel garden's design details with curving brick paths, a central turf event space, and pavilion-style access points to the underground garage. Geofoam layers created undulating mounds, while concrete pavers contained the 6-inch gravel layer, delineated adjoining gardens, and served as a mowing strip for adjacent turf.

OPPOSITE As software company Epic continues to grow, the campus gardens at its Wisconsin headquarters help cultivate creativity for its 14,000 employees. The gravel garden is one of many eco-conscious gardens throughout its five campuses that employees, visiting customers, and the community enjoy.

When envisioning landscape plantings for an expansive 3-acre rooftop garden at software company Epic's headquarters, Jeff Epping found inspiration in the idea of a gravel garden. "The roof of this underground parking garage had shallow soil and weight restrictions, so it ruled out tree plantings and water-thirsty plants," says Jeff. "A gravel garden seemed like the perfect solution." The central lawn serves as special event space for company picnics, summer farmers' markets, group yoga sessions, and even an occasional game of kickball.

Jeff meticulously curated the plant lists tailored to each garden section's theme. The horticulture team then sourced the plants in quart-size pots and oversaw their care on-site until installation day. The installation involved a team of ten members plus additional seasonal staff. A few team members placed the 65,000 plants while others followed with floral shovels, digging holes in the gravel layer and installing the plants. They arranged a diverse mix of native prairie plants like coneflowers, coreopsis, baptisia, and penstemon among grasses like prairie dropseed and little bluestem.

"Our goal was not to see the gravel in three years," says Jackie. So, they densely spaced plants, no more than 18 inches apart from one plant center to the next.

Since the gardens were installed in the heat of summer (not to mention a very exposed, windy location), the new plants were initially watered two to three times per day. They were slowly weaned off the irrigation as their roots grew more deeply into the well-draining engineered soil. After the first year, the gardens were only watered in extreme droughts.

"Some years, we've needed no irrigation at all," says Jackie.

While the maintenance is definitely less compared to traditional landscaping, the annual cleanup remains an important and significant endeavor.

"There's big maintenance at the beginning and the end, but during the season there's not a lot of maintenance," says Zane Fuller, Epic horticulturist in charge of the gravel gardens.

He coordinates two cutbacks. In fall, the team focuses exclusively on cutting back the prairie dropseed, using soil knives to remove the drooping foliage. They learned to wait until early spring to remove the remainder of plant material, since the foliage protects plant crowns from harsh winter conditions and provides winter cover for wildlife.

In March, the team starts at one corner of the garden and works its way across to the opposite corner. Half the team uses electric hedge trimmers to cut foliage to the ground, while the balance follows to rake the material and load it on a trailer attached to a utility vehicle. The material is then moved to the company's farm where it is composted. The two cutbacks typically take three to four days and require 300 to 400 staff-hours (equating to two hours and twenty minutes per 1000 square feet).

"It's typically the first project with our seasonal crew and a collaborative one we work on together before everyone heads in different directions for the rest of the season," says Zane.

Over the years, the team gleaned valuable insights, especially the importance of plant variety.

"Diversity is a good thing," says Jackie. "You don't want too much of one thing, or you could end up with big empty spots if plants fail."

They also learned the necessity of gravel that is washed of finer particles and maintains air spaces between individual pieces of gravel to mitigate weed issues. In Juno, Epic's Southwestern-themed garden, they discovered that the red gravel mulch used to create the look of a barren arid landscape (not a gravel garden) unfortunately became the perfect medium for weed seeds to thrive. The fines between the gravel held ample water for seeds to germinate and grow.

The rooftop also has had its own nuances for plants. Over the years, they've discovered the most success with extremely drought-tolerant plants like blazing star (*Liatris aspera*), prairie dropseed (*Sporobolus heterolepis*), little bluestem (*Schizachyrium scoparium*), pale purple coneflower (*Echinacea pallida*), and yellow coneflower (*Echinacea paradoxa*). Other plants like catmint (*Nepeta racemosa*) and purple coneflower (*Echinacea purpurea*) have not held up well since they don't produce deep root systems necessary to survive in the extremely exposed site. Voles devoured the purple love grass (*Eragrostis spectabilis*), and rabbits consumed the skyblue asters (*Symphyotrichum oolentangiense*).

Epic's six campuses are cared for by a team of 20 plus an additional 20 seasonal staff. Originally the team worked together on all aspects of the garden. As they have grown, team members now specialize in turf, site management, new project installations, or campus horticulture.

"The gravel gardens are my favorite part of this campus," says Zane. "I love watching all the prairie plants change through the seasons and all the wildlife they attract—even endangered bumblebees and butterflies are found on campus." He says it's rewarding to have this diversity of plants in the middle of a software-technology campus and to have fellow employees stop to ask questions and express gratitude.

No doubt, the gravel gardens complement Epic's overall sustainability initiatives. Most parking spaces are underground, reducing the company's footprint and preserving the idyllic countryside. The headquarters' 28 office buildings are heated and cooled by thousands of miles of geothermal pipes reaching 500 feet underground. The campus also uses green energy, including six wind turbines and 18 acres of solar panels.

As Epic continues to grow, its gardens play a role in staff retention and recruiting, cultivating a creative and productive environment for its 14,000 employees, and creating welcoming spaces for visiting customers and community members.

"Anytime we can show different ways of doing things, it's a positive," says Jackie. "We're a resource like a botanic garden to inspire others."

ABOVE Jackie Hager, Epic's long-tenured horticulturist; Zane Fuller, horticulturist responsible for the gravel gardens; and Jeff Epping are instrumental in the gravel garden's design and ongoing care. "The gravel gardens are my favorite part of this campus," says Zane. "I love watching all the prairie plants change through the seasons and all the wildlife they attract--even endangered bumblebees and butterflies are found on campus." He says it's rewarding to have this diversity of plants in the middle of a software-technology campus and to have fellow employees stop to ask questions and express gratitude.

Benefits of a Gravel Garden Green Roof

Green roofs vary widely in their construction and plant makeup and provide a unique opportunity to cool our planet. Gravel gardens are best grown in a minimum 12 inches of deep-growing medium that is topped with 4 to 6 inches of washed gravel (¼-inch or similarly sized) over a waterproof membrane and drainage system to take away excess water. Between buildings and parking garages, Epic now supports 35 acres of green roof gardens.

AESTHETICS: The greening of a roof offers visual appeal in urban settings and an enhanced view from many office buildings.

STORMWATER MANAGEMENT: Green roofs reduce the amount and slow down the rate of stormwater runoff, resulting in decreased stress on sewer systems. In summer, green roofs retain 70 to 90 percent of the precipitation that falls on them. In winter, retention is 25 to 40 percent.

MODERATION OF URBAN HEAT: The dew and evaporation of green roof plants help cool cities during hot summer months and reduce the Urban Heat Island (UHI). Green roof temperatures can be 30 to 40 degrees Fahrenheit lower than those of conventional roofs and can reduce citywide ambient temperatures by up to 5 degrees Fahrenheit. (Source: EPA "Using Green Roofs to Reduce Heat Islands.")

IMPROVED AIR QUALITY: Plants on green roofs capture airborne pollutants and filter noxious gases.

ENERGY EFFICIENCY: Green roofs provide insulation and reduce the amount of energy needed to moderate the temperature of a building. Research by the National Research Council Canada found that an extensive green roof reduced the daily energy demand for air-conditioning in summer by more than 75 percent.

FIRE RETARDATION: Green roofs have lower burning heat load (the heat generated when a substance burns) than do conventional roofs.

INCREASED BIODIVERSITY: Green roofs can sustain a variety of plants and invertebrates and provide habitat for various bird species. By acting as a stepping-stone habitat for migrating birds, they can link species together that would otherwise be fragmented.

LEARN MORE: For online training courses, resources, and a directory of green roof professionals, visit www.greenroofs.org.

The allure of reduced maintenance made gravel gardens an appealing choice for Epic despite their untested nature in such a large space--and on a roof to boot. Landscape architect Linda Sievert fleshed out the gravel garden's design details with curving brick paths, a central turf event space, and pavilion-style access points to the underground garage. Lightweight geofoam layers created undulating mounds, while concrete pavers contained the 6-inch gravel layer, delineated adjoining gardens, and served as a mowing strip for adjacent turf.

Splendid Silhouettes

1 Adam's needle (*Yucca filamentosa*) seed capsules are quite ornamental in the fall and winter. **2 Common milkweed** (*Asclepias syriaca*) seed pods burst as they dry in fall, and silked seed floats away to start new colonies downwind. **3 Tickseed** (*Coreopsis palmata*) and its small, scaly seed capsules are produced in abundance and visited by hungry goldfinches that relish their tiny black seeds. **4 Switch grass** (*Panicum virgatum*) blades and seed heads sway gently in the wind and give the garden movement and life. **5** The locally sourced ¼- to ⅜-inch washed chipped quartzite gravel is spread across the gardens 4 to 5 inches deep. The uniformly sized gravel chips are key to weed suppression; they maintain air pockets between each chip, creating an environment too dry for most seeds to germinate. **6 Little bluestem** (*Schizachyrium scoparium*) and its coppery seed stalks with contrasting white seed spikelets are not only beautiful for our enjoyment but essential food for small songbirds like field sparrows and juncos. **7 Wild quinine** (*Parthenium integrifolium*) seed heads are as ornamental in their brown stage as they are in their summer white. **8 Smooth aster** (*Symphyotrichum laeve*) dried flower stems shed their silky seeds. The cultivar 'Bluebird' ranked #1 in Mt. Cuba Center's aster trials. **9 Pale purple coneflower** (*Echinacea pallida*) seed heads are one of the best for winter interest in the garden while providing seeds for goldfinches when they need it most.

OPPOSITE: TOP LEFT Yucca stems are allowed to stand sculpturally in the fall and winter garden. The evergreen foliage is nice in contrast to the brown tones around the garden. The broad overlapping leaves also protect plant crowns from harsh winter conditions while providing winter cover for wildlife. **TOP RIGHT** Over the years, Jackie has come to appreciate diversity in the gravel gardens. "You don't want too much of one thing, or you could end up with big empty spots if plants fail," she says. **BOTTOM LEFT** Zane coordinates two cutbacks--one in fall to selectively trim drooping foliage and the major one in spring. **BOTTOM RIGHT** Prairie blazing star (*Liatris pycnostachya*) and its tall fluffy flower stalks elegantly dance across the gravel garden and provide seed for black-capped chickadees later in the season.

The design called for a diverse mix of species--all needed to be as cold-hardy and drought-tolerant as possible, since the roof's weight restrictions only allowed for 12 to 18 inches of soil depth. Planted above several thousand cars, the garden includes 65,000 plants--many native prairie species like coneflowers, coreopsis, baptisia, and penstemon, among grasses like prairie dropseed and little bluestem.

"Our goal was to cover the gravel in three years," says Jackie. So, they densely spaced plants, no more than 18 inches apart from one plant center to the next. Bush clovers were planted for their floral impact in early fall when Epic hosts Users Group Meeting (UGM), its biggest annual event. 'Gibraltar' Thunberg bush clover (*Lespedeza thunbergii* 'Gibraltar') (left) is a large shrub with cascading branches with gorgeous pink flowers. It is extremely drought-tolerant--perfect for a large-scale gravel garden. Western bumblebees are enjoying another great fall bloomer with a well-behaved, non-running habit: 'Wichita Mountains' goldenrod (*Solidago* 'Wichita Mountains') (above), an absolute pollinator magnet in the garden.

Epic occupies over 1500 acres (410 acres of campus, 750 acres of active farmland) in Verona, Wisconsin, just 12 miles from Madison. Nearly all of Epic's 10,000 parking spaces are underground, with planted gardens on top. If this were all surface parking, they'd have approximately 90 acres of impermeable asphalt. Instead of asphalt and cars baking in the sun, Epic chose coneflowers and other plants, wildlife habitat, rainwater infiltration, heat reduction, and beautiful parklike spaces for their employees to enjoy.

ARGONNE NATIONAL LABORATORY
Lemont, Illinois

Sustainable Statement

Located in a forest preserve 25 miles west of Chicago, Argonne National Laboratory is a research powerhouse tackling issues like climate change and green energy. When it came to landscaping the expanded Theory and Computing Sciences Building (TCS), which houses the new Aurora supercomputer, one of the largest and fastest in the world, the team of researchers and scientists working there chose a visionary approach that mirrored its innovative spirit: gravel gardens.

Designed by landscape architect David Yocca, FASLA (Solutions in the Land), and plantsman Roy Diblik (Northwind Perennial Farm), the ⅔-acre gardens offer a welcoming and sustainable entrance for scientists visiting from around the world. Installed in 2021, the centerpiece is an island gravel garden bursting with prairie grasses and colorful flowering perennials. More gravel gardens wrap around the atrium lobby, outdoor café, and glass-fronted meeting rooms, offering peaceful views of textural grasses interspersed with tough, flowering perennials.

The TCS team sought a departure from traditional, high-maintenance landscapes, for one that was authentic to DuPage County, Illinois. Inspired by Roy's creation at Northwind Perennial Farm, David proposed gravel gardens.

"They didn't want a traditional, highly manicured, chemically dependent landscape," says David. "Instead, they wanted an immersive, naturalistic garden that aligned with the lab's work in climate and energy research and connected with Waterfall Glen, a forest preserve that surrounds the campus."

David had visited Roy's gravel garden several years ago and dreamed of one day installing one together. He learned from Roy how he had been wowed by a visit to Cassian Schmidt's gravel gardens at Hermannshof Garden in Germany and returned home to create his own in 2006. Roy followed Cassian's model, spreading the essential 5-inch layer of gravel in a 200-square-foot plot and adding in ten tough prairie plants, resulting in a water-free, weed-free garden in just a year.

"The lean concept made so much sense, and I finally had a chance to try one at Argonne," says David.

Initially, the TSCB team took a bit of convincing, having experienced weed issues with a previous seeded meadow. David addressed their concerns by arranging a tour of the 3-acre gravel garden at Epic Systems headquarters two hours north in Verona, Wisconsin. He also presented cost projections demonstrating significant long-term savings compared to traditional landscape with weekly mowings, lawn treatments, weeding, and pruning. The team was convinced.

David, with support from VIRIDIS Design Group (a landscape design firm in Michigan), went on to lay out a master plan, maximizing resources and impact while prioritizing the entrance area. He factored in interior and exterior sight lines from the atrium lobby, glass-walled corridor, and conference rooms. His design incorporated outcropping stones, rivers of boulders, and cobble edges, reminiscent of the adjacent Waterfall Glen preserve.

"It's an abstract version of nature within the built outdoor space," explains David.

OPPOSITE The gravel gardens at Argonne National Laboratory's new supercomputer facility effectively demonstrate the power of sustainable design. They provide a beautiful, low-maintenance landscape that reflects the research powerhouse's commitment to environmental stewardship.

The 2/3-acre gravel garden offers a welcoming and sustainable entrance for scientists visiting from around the world. “The benefits of connecting people with nature are infinite, and we must be more open minded to integrate truly living landscapes in creative ways into our workplaces, our homes, our schools, and our cities,” says landscape architect and project leader David Yocca.

STOP

Finding a qualified contractor for the installation and maintenance was crucial to the garden's success. David and the site development team, led by Turner Construction (a global construction company), interviewed several and chose locally based Atrium Landscape.

"We spent a lot of time focusing on the maintenance part," says David. "We made sure to have an experienced landscape contractor in place that really understood the concept and how to care for and steward the landscapes once fully established," he says.

While requiring less maintenance, gravel gardens still need care at a few critical stages every year.

"It's not zero maintenance," says David, who says young plants needed to be watered initially until their roots are established. While there's no weekly mowing, shearing shrubs, mulching, edging, or weeding, spring cleanup is imperative. Herbaceous plants must be cut back and removed before they break down and produce organic matter, offering a place for weeds to grow.

Atrium's team meticulously prepared the site. They cleared the existing vegetation and added compost to the soil.

"We had some very shallow utilities and couldn't really dig deep and rip up the soil because a whole network of electrical and communications infrastructure (300 miles of cabling) was right underneath," says David. They strategically placed eastern white pine and swamp, white, bur, and red oaks in pockets as another nod to the nearby preserve reference landscapes. Next, they followed Roy's method, spreading 5 inches of gravel within the boundaries of the building, driveway curb, walkways, and stacked limestone borders and walls. All of these different types of edge borders are important in maintaining the gravel depth along the edges of the garden.

"It's a process style," says Roy. "You can't cheat the 5-inch layer, or you lose with weeds pushing through more shallow areas."

David also leaned on Roy and his wife, Annamaria Leon, for the herbaceous plant selection. They assembled a list of plants with "durability and a forgiving nature," calculated quantities by assigning percentages to each plant, then ordered a total of 6000 plants to fill the space. The most dominant plants, 2600 prairie dropseeds, serve as a base layer for the diverse mix.

"I was inspired by Jeff's boldness in plant choices," says Roy about Jeff's work at Olbrich Botanical Gardens. "So I've expanded my palette beyond my favorite hill prairie plants to add yarrows and pale purple coneflowers that also thrive in the well-drained gravel."

In August, Roy and Annamaria along with their design friend Austin Eischeid arranged the plant plugs on-site. The Atrium team followed, planting the plugs into the gravel with instructions interpreted in Spanish by Annamaria.

Roy describes his spontaneous design process as emotional. He planted drifts of ruby red switch grass and purple Russian sage crossing from one bed to the next. In between, he interspersed colorful yellow and red coneflowers. Closer to the building's concrete walls, he planted taller mauve joe-pye weed and deep purple, big bluestem with feather reed grasses in front.

For the next six weeks, the contractor's crew hand-watered the new plants every three days. Each watering took 25 hours. They returned the following spring to fill in additional plants and install an irrigation system to more cost-effectively water new plants and use as a future backup in case of extreme drought.

The gravel gardens at Argonne effectively demonstrate the power of sustainable design adapted to the specific needs and desires of client and site. They provide a beautiful, low-maintenance landscape that reflects Argonne's commitment to environmental stewardship. The gardens not only enhance the aesthetics of the workplace but also serve as a testament to the innovative spirit that fuels scientific discovery at Argonne.

"The benefits of connecting people with nature are infinite, and we must be more open-minded to integrate truly living landscapes in creative ways into our workplaces, our homes, our schools, and our cities," says David.

OPPOSITE David Yocca stands on the natural limestone boulders, whose tops he had saw-cut to function as both garden seating and soil retention.

Late-Fall Performers

❶ **Autumn moor grass** (*Sesleria autumnalis*) flowers turn dark brown in autumn, contrasting beautifully against the lime-green foliage as it takes on gold fall color. ❷ **Beard-tongue** (*Penstemon digitalis*) in full fall color. A plant of every season, it has beautiful white and pale violet flowers in late spring that form showy burgundy seed heads in summer. ❸ **Hyssop-leaf thoroughwort** (*Eupatorium hyssopifolium*) is one of the latest fall-blooming perennials. Its frothy white flowers attract pollinators by the hundreds. ❹ **'Summer's Swan Song' ironweed** (*Vernonia* × 'Summer's Swan Song') blooms for five to six weeks in mid- to late fall, when few other perennials are still flowering and are highly attractive to pollinators, especially migrating monarchs. Strong sturdy stems turn from green to dark red after the flowers fade, adding even more fall interest. ❺ Locally sourced washed pea gravel, applied 5 inches thick, prevents weed seeds from germinating. ❻ **'October Skies'** aromatic aster (*Symphyotrichum oblongifolium* 'October Skies') in full bloom in late fall, often flowers right up until a hard frost. This vigorous grower is tough as nails and very deer- and rabbit-resistant. ❼ **'Red October'** big bluestem (*Andropogon gerardii* 'Red October') is a shorter, strong-stemmed cultivar of one of our most beautiful native prairie grasses. An added bonus is that much of its deep green foliage takes on red hues as the season progresses and intensifies to rich burgundy by late fall. ❽ Nurseryman and plant designer Roy Diblik is known for his brilliant perennial plant designs crafted of native and non-native species that live in community with each other. ❾ **'Ruby Ribbons' switch grass** (*Panicum virgatum* 'Ruby Ribbons') is a short-statured cultivar of our native prairie species with blue-green foliage that takes on fiery red tones in late summer and fall. ❿ **Russian sage** (*Perovskia atriplicifolia*), rattlesnake master (*Eryngium yuccifolium*), feather reed grass (*Calamagrostis* × *acutiflora* 'Karl Foerster'), and

7

8

9

10

11

12

other fine-textured perennials were chosen by plant designer Roy Diblik to soften the hard concrete walls of the building. 11 **'Little Spire' Russian sage** (*Perovskia atriplicifolia* 'Little Spire') has flowers that shimmer in the sunlight. Few plant species are as drought-tolerant and beautiful, and there are a multitude of excellent cultivars of varying heights and widths, including the more upright and compact growing 'Little Spire'. 12 **'American Gold Rush' black-eyed Susan** (*Rudbeckia* × 'American Gold Rush') is a compact, heat-tolerant, disease-resistant cultivar that excels in most sunny conditions, including gravel gardens.

Taking advantage of the glass walls of indoor rooms and hallways, David seamlessly connected the building's interior to the landscape, designing gardens completely around the atrium lobby, outdoor café, and meeting rooms to offer serene garden views in every season.

Throughout the garden, seating areas were designed to offer a place for visitors and associates to sit and enjoy the wide diversity of plants and the creatures they support, from insects and birds to reptiles and small mammals.

STOP

The Prairie Rainwater Parkway Garden

In 2023, David Yocca, Roy Diblik and his wife, horticulturist Annamaria Leon, collaborated with Blacks in Green (BIG), a Chicago-based environmental-justice organization, to install two parkway gravel gardens at the Mamie Till-Mobley Forgiveness Garden in the West Woodlawn neighborhood south of the city. Called the Prairie Rainwater Parkway Garden, this project is a low-maintenance and cost-effective approach to urban green spaces.

"I thought these small spaces would be the perfect place to experiment with gravel gardens," says David, who serves as green infrastructure director for BIG. "Since maintenance resources are so limited, the gravel gardens are much more cost-effective than typical, more intensive perennial gardens and allow us a level of beauty, biodiversity, and enjoyment that the community couldn't have had otherwise."

BIG secured grants from the Trust for Public Land to support the development of the garden site, including accessible, permeable walking paths, with additional funding and volunteer support from the footwear company Timberland for the initial two gravel gardens.

These two gravel gardens transformed 8-foot-by-25-foot parkway strips (between the sidewalk and the curb) into vibrant arrival features for the Forgiveness Garden. The parkways, already planted with trees from a 2021 BIG tree-planting initiative, were prepped by removing turfgrass, loosening the soil, and amending with compost. A 5-inch gravel layer was then spread, contained by a border of larger flagstones.

On June 19, volunteers from the community and a team of Timberland employees planted 800 plants in the gravel. The chosen plants, including ornamental onion, threadleaf coreopsis, coneflowers, gayfeather, and prairie dropseed, thrive in this low-water environment. They wrapped up the planting with a Juneteenth community celebration.

The Forgiveness Garden honors Mamie Till-Mobley, a courageous mother and activist. Her insistence on an open-casket funeral for her fourteen-year-old son Emmett, brutally lynched in Mississippi in 1955, became a powerful catalyst for the Civil Rights Movement.

This parkway project is part of BIG's larger initiative, the Great Migration Greenway. The greenway transforms vacant lots into gardens honoring neighborhood heroes of the Great Migration while simultaneously enhancing the West Woodlawn neighborhood's climate resilience.

"These greenway gardens are absorbing rainwater, providing cooling, and offering pollinator habitat," says David.

BIG's rejuvenation plans continue. Six more parkway gravel gardens are planned for the neighborhood. And the garden is part of a local and regional climate change study by Argonne National Laboratory through their CROCUS (Community Research on Climate and Urban Science) initiative. The study explores how urban elements like trees, green spaces, buildings, and Lake Michigan influence Chicago's climate. The study's findings will empower communities to build resilience for the future.

ABOVE In 2023, David and Roy collaborated with Chicago's Blacks in Green (BIG) to install two parkway gravel gardens at the Mamie Till-Mobley Forgiveness Garden in South Chicago. The garden is part of a local and regional climate change study by Argonne National Laboratory.

‘Baby Swan White’ coneflowers (*Echinacea purpurea* ‘Baby Swan White’) and plains oval sedge (*Carex brevior*) are two tough plants selected for this low-water environment.

Argonne's Theory and Computing Sciences Building is home to Aurora exascale supercomputer, one of the world's fastest computers, running 2 billion billion calculations per second, allowing scientists to accelerate studies in climate change, earth evolution, weather modeling, drug design, and airplane safety. The gravel gardens designed by David Yocca and Roy Diblik reflect Argonne's vision of seeking "scientific and engineering solutions to the grand challenges of our time: sustainable energy, a healthy environment, and a secure nation."

ACKNOWLEDGMENTS

I extend my deepest gratitude to co-author Jeff Epping, who invited me to join him on this incredible book project. At first, I was intimidated by Jeff's vast horticulture experience, but I quickly discovered what a joy he is to work with—so welcoming, generous with his knowledge, and genuinely interested in everyone he meets. He is a cultivator of both plants and people as well as a true champion for more sustainable gardening.

To the wonderfully inventive and creative gravel gardeners featured in these pages, it was an absolute privilege to interview and learn from you. Your generosity in sharing your stories, innovative approaches, enthusiasm, and deep plant wisdom has enriched this book in countless ways.

Our heartfelt appreciation goes to the talented team at Timber Press, especially executive editor Makenna Goodman. Her invaluable feedback, encouragement, and leadership helped shape this book from concept to reality. A special thanks also to Bob Stefko, whose stunning photography captures the essence of the fifteen U.S. gardens with his unmatched storytelling ability and work ethic.

Finally, to my husband, Brian, and our children, Brittany, Rachel, and Mark—thank you for your love and encouragement and for inspiring me with your own pursuits. Your support means everything.

—Teresa Woodard

A heartfelt thanks to my friends who shared their extraordinary gardens and stories with us. Your commitment—from preparing your gardens for us and dedicating time from dawn till dusk for photo shoots, participating in interviews, helping identify plants, and meticulously reviewing chapter drafts—was instrumental in bringing this book to life. Your artistry, passion, and tireless efforts have resulted in some of the most inspiring, thoughtful, and beautiful gardens I've had the pleasure to experience.

To my parents, who instilled in me the love of nature and plants, taught me the value of hard work, and supported my horticultural aspirations—I know they are proudly watching over this achievement. And to all my brothers and sisters, who've encouraged me along the way.

My deepest appreciation goes to my wife, Kathy, for her unwavering support throughout this endeavor and countless others. Without her, balancing these projects and family life would not have been possible. To our children, Griffin, Kara, and Keegan—your zest for life and personal achievements continually inspire me.

To my Olbrich family, with whom I spent over twenty-eight years helping transform an infant, lawn-dominated botanic garden into one of the nation's finest public gardens. Special thanks to visionary director Nancy Ragland for believing in a very green horticulturist, and to the talented and passionate team of gardeners I had the honor to lead and collaborate with over the years—we created something truly special together.

To my many friends and colleagues in the horticultural community—your creativity, dedication, and generosity in sharing your knowledge have been a source of inspiration and pivotal in advancing our craft to create a better world through the art of gardening. A heartfelt thank you to my mentor and friend, professor Edward Hasselkus, whose insightful guidance from my college degrees to this day has been a cornerstone of my professional journey.

To my exceptional partners on this project—Teresa Woodard, whose wordsmithing brought our vision to life, and Bob Stefko, whose artistic eye added depth and beauty—you both made this endeavor more enjoyable than I ever imagined. Your combined experience, unwavering work ethic, and camaraderie navigated us through the complexities of this journey with remarkable ease.

A special thank you to the brilliant team at Timber Press, including Makenna Goodman, associate director of publicity Katlynn Nicolls, and publicist Melina Dorrance, for working with Teresa, Bob, and me to bring this book to life. A shout out to Nick and Allison McCullough for their encouragement and help in initiating this project with Timber Press.

Finally, thank you to everyone designing and cultivating ecologically conscious spaces that address our struggling ecosystems and the challenges posed by our changing climate—together, through the power of plants and gardens, we will make a meaningful difference for future generations.

—Jeff Epping

PHOTO CREDITS

All photos are by Bob Stefko, except for the following:

Adam Glas, 101 (right)
Andrew Bunting, 73 (bottom)
Bettina Jaugstetter, 144 (top, bottom right), 145
Cassian Schmidt, 137–139, 141 (top left, bottom), 142, 143, 144 (bottom left), 146–149
Charlie Burrell, 267 (top, bottom left), 268, 271–273
Charlie Harpur, 267 (bottom right), 269, 270
Chris Abraham, 128
Jared Barnes, 216
Jeff Epping, 18–23, 24 (bottom left), 114, 141 (top right), 282 (left), 286, 287, 297 (top right)
Julie Skelton, 227–230, 231 (inset), 232–235
Karen Finley, 266 (left)
Lisa Roper, 94–95, 106–107, 189 (top right), 192–195
Richard Bloom, 261–265, 266 (right)

Alamy

Elizabeth Whiting & Associates, 243
Faiz Balabil, 237, 242, 345 (left, top right), 244, 246, 244, 246–247
Gareth Fuller, 257
Keith Mindham, 231 (main)
John Cole, 241 (inset)
Lynn Hilton, 238–239
Maddie Thornhill, 241 (main)
Sophie Davidson, 245 (bottom right)

©National Trust Images

Annaick Guitteny, 255
Eva Nemeth, 250–251, 258–259
James Dobson, 249, 253, 254
Pearson Studio, 256

Recommended Reading

Chatto, Beth, *Beth Chatto's Gravel Garden: Drought-Resistant Planting Through the Year*, Avery Publishing, 2000.

Chatto, Beth and Steven Wooster, *Drought-Resistant Planting: Lessons from Beth Chatto's Gravel Garden*, Frances Lincoln Publishing, 2016.

Diblik, Roy, *The Know Maintenance Perennial Garden*, Timber Press, 2014.

Diboll, Neil and Hilary Cox, *The Gardener's Guide to Prairie Plants*, University of Chicago Press, 2023.

Filippi, Olivier, *The Dry Gardening Handbook: Plants and Practices for a Changing Climate*, Filbert Press, 2019.

Filippi, Olivier, *Planting Design for Dry Gardens: Beautiful, Resilient Groundcovers for Terraces, Paved Areas, Gravel and Other Alternatives to the Lawn*, Filbert Press, 2016.

Holm, Heather, *Pollinators of Native Plants: Attract, Observe and Identify Pollinators and Beneficial Insects with Native Plants*, Pollination Press, 2014.

Jarman, Derek, Howard Sooley, and Jamaica Kincaid, *Derek Jarman's Garden: 30th Anniversary Edition*, Timber Press, 2025.

McCullough, Nick, Allison McCullough, and Teresa Woodard, *American Roots: Lessons and Inspiration from the Designers Reimagining Our Home Gardens*, Timber Press, 2022.

Norris, Kelly D., *New Naturalism: Designing and Planting a Resilient, Ecologically Vibrant Home Garden*, Cool Springs Press, 2021.

Norris, Kelly D., *Your Natural Garden: A Practical Guide to Caring for an Ecologically Vibrant Home Garden*, Cool Springs Press, 2025.

Oudolf, Piet, and Noel Kingsbury, *Planting: A New Perspective*, Timber Press, 2013.

Rainer, Thomas and Claudia West, *Planting in a Post-Wild World: Designing Plant Communities for Resilient Landscapes*, Timber Press, 2015.

Raven, Sarah, and Vita Sackville-West, *Vita Sackville-West's Sissinghurst: The Creation of a Garden*, Virago Press, 2014.

Tallamy, Douglas W., *Nature's Best Hope: A New Approach to Conservation That Starts in Your Yard*, Timber Press, 2019.

Thomas, R. William, *The Art of Gardening: Design Inspiration and Innovative Planting Techniques from Chanticleer*, Timber Press, 2015.

Tree, Isabella and Charlie Burrell, *The Book of Wilding: A Practical Guide to Rewilding, Big and Small*, Bloomsbury Publishing, 2023.

Woodard, Teresa, and Bob Stefko, *Gardens to the Max: Joyful, Visionary, Maximalist Design*, Timber Press, 2025.

Online Resources

Bunting, Andrew, "Andrew Bunting of the Pennsylvania Horticultural Society," Garden Masterclass, YouTube, May 8, 2020. Polly Hill Arboretum Lecture, YouTube, May 27, 2022.

Diblik, Roy, "Gravel Gardening! What a Concept!! Episode #119," YouTube, Sept. 22, 2021.

Glas, Adam, "Gardener's Almanac: May 31 - Planting in Gravel Culture," Scott Arboretum & Gardens, YouTube, June 4, 2021.

Illinois Wildflowers Native Plant Database, www.illinoiswildflowers.info.

Lady Bird Johnson Wildflower Center Native Plants Database, www.wildflower.org/plants.

Missouri Botanical Garden Plant Finder, www.missouribotanicalgarden.org/plantfinder/plantfindersearch.aspx.

Mt. Cuba Center Trial Garden, Sam Hoadley, Mt. Cuba Center, www.mtcubacenter.org/research/trial-garden.

O'Brien, Ben, Wild by Design, www.wildbydesign.ca.

Plant Evaluation Notes, Richard Hawke, Chicago Botanic Garden, www.chicagobotanic.org/collections/ornamental_plant_research/plant_evaluation.

Roper, Lisa, "Lisa Roper in Chanticleer's Gravel Garden," Garden Masterclass, Vimeo, July 30, 2020.

Schmidt, Cassian, "Ecology Based Maintenance Regimes for Perennial Style Plantings with Cassian Schmidt," Garden Masterclass, Vimeo, March 28, 2022.

Gardens and Garden Designers

Abraham, Chris – www.72seasons.garden

Argonne National Laboratory – www.anl.gov

Barnes, Jared. Meristem and plant•ed – meristemhorticulture.com

Beth Chatto's Plants & Gardens – www.bethchatto.co.uk

Bunting, Andrew – www.phsonline.org/team/andrew-bunting

Chanticleer – www.chanticleergarden.org

Diblik, Roy. Roy Diblik Perennial Garden Design – www.roydiblik.com

Epic Systems – www.epic.com/visiting

Epping, Jeff. Jeff Epping Design & Consulting – www.jeffepping.com

Glas, Adam – www.scottarboretum.org

Hitchmough, James – www.sheffield.ac.uk/architecture-landscape/people/academic/james-hitchmough

Knepp Castle Estate – www.knepp.co.uk/knepp-estate/gardens

Lyon, Edward. Spellbound Garden Writing & Consultation – www.spellboundgarden.org

Norris, Kelly D. – www.kellydnorris.com

Olbrich Botanical Gardens – www.olbrich.org

Pearson, Dan. Dan Pearson Studio – www.danpearsonstudio.com

PHS Meadowbrook Farm – www.phsonline.org/locations/phs-meadowbrook-farm

Prospect Cottage – www.creativefolkestone.org.uk/prospect-cottage

Reiman Gardens – www.reimangardens.com

Roper, Lisa – www.lisaroper.com

Sissinghurst Castle Garden, Delos Garden – www.nationaltrust.org.uk/visit/kent/sissinghurst-castle-garden/recreating-delos-at-sissinghurst

Stephen F. Austin University – www.sfasu.edu

Stuart-Smith, Tom – www.tomstuartsmith.co.uk

The Scott Arboretum of Swarthmore College – www.scottarboretum.org

Yocca, David – www.linkedin.com/in/davidyocca

INDEX

A
ABB, 140, 142
Abraham, Chris, 122, 126, 133
Acanthus spinosus, 174
accessibility, 202
achillea, 136
Achillea × 'Moonshine', 130
Achillea coarctata, 256
Achillea 'Feuerland', 25
Adam's needle, 158, 216, 284
Adopt A Lot program, 8–9, 122–135
aesthetics, 36, 202, 282
African daisy, 236
'Afterglow' Mexican hens and chicks hybrid, 191
Agastache 'Blue Fortune', 204
Agastache 'Kudos Mandarin', 204
Agastache 'Linda', 84
Agastache 'Queen Nectarine', 176
Agastache rugosa, 84
Agastache rupestris, 84
agave, 62, 180
Agave americana, 188
Agave attenuata 'Variegata', 188
Agave parryi 'J.C. Raulston', 71
ageratum, 76
air pollution, 128
Allen Centennial Garden, 196
allium, 62, 66, 112, 126, 158, 184, 196
Allium × 'New Moon', 131, 133
Allium cernuum, 161
Allium karataviense 'Ivory Queen', 193, 195
Allium lusitanicum 'Summer Beauty', 24, 117, 160
Allium 'Millenium', 70, 204
Allium 'Purple Sensation', 102, 106
Alluaudia procera, 191
Aloe marlothii, 191
American basketflwoer, 84
American century plant, 188
'American Gold Rush' black-eyed Susan, 297
Ames, IA, 9, 30–45, 196–209
Amorpha canescens, 116
amsonia, 46, 55, 112, 120, 196, 199
Amsonia ciliata var. *tenuifolia* 'Georgia Pancake', 174
Amsonia hubrichtii, 58, 73, 206
Anaphalis margaritacea, 70
Andropogon gerardii 'Holy Smoke', 42
Andropogon gerardii 'Red October', 296
anise hyssop, 196, 199
annual fleabane, 265
annual honesty, 256
annuals, 16, 100, 155, 219
Appalachian mountain mint, 102
Argonne National Laboratory, 9, 122, 290–305
aromatic aster, 217
art, 25, 36
Artemisia ludoviciana 'Garden Ghost', 130
Artemisia 'Powis Castle', 192
Art Fund, 240
Asclepias syriaca, 184
Asclepias tuberosa, 24, 38, 103, 160
Asclepias verticillata, 38
Ashton, Glenn, 8, 166–179
Asian spicebush, 73
Asian Woods, 180
Asphodeline lutea, 195
aster, 12, 46, 55, 62, 92, 96, 126, 156, 158, 195, 210, 214
Atlas mountain daisy, 256
Atrium Landscape, 294
autumn moor grass, 24, 296

B
baby's breath, 166, 168
'Baby Swan White' coneflower, 303
Ballota pseudodictamnus, 256
baptisia, 286
bare-rooting, 101
Barnes, Jared, 8, 84, 210–224
beaked yucca, 166, 180
beardtongue, 46, 55, 156, 296
bear's breeches, 174
beautyberry, 62
'Beavertail' cactus, 180, 188
bee balm, 46, 55, 58, 126, 152, 216
bees, 16, 27, 70, 116, 133, 161
beetles, 260
Benarcik, Dan, 73
benches, 73, 82, 202
Beth Chatto Education Trust, 230
Beth Chatto Gardens, 7, 9, 226–235
Beth Chatto's Garden Tapestry (Chatto), 230

Beth Chatto's Gravel Garden (Chatto), 226
betony, 76
biennials, 188
big bluestem, 16, 76, 112, 180, 294
'Big Ears' lamb's ears, 204
biodiversity, 50, 128, 253, 282
birds, 12, 50, 76, 156, 218, 271, 300
BLACKBIRD spurge, 71
black-capped chickadee, 284
black-eyed Susan, 34, 39, 46, 55, 112, 120, 155, 156, 196, 199
Blacks in Green (BIG), 302
blazing star, 92, 103, 105, 133, 280
bluebonnet, 214
'Blue Fortune' giant hyssop, 204
blue gama grass, 196, 199
'Blue Glitter' sea holly, 188
'BLUE HEAVEN' little bluestem, 102
blue myrtle cactus, 191
'Blue Ribbons' clematis, 184
blue star, 73, 92
bluestem, 85
bluet damselfly, 161
blue-winged wasp, 128
Boler, Leo, 126
Bolz Conservatory, 152, 156
Bombus affinis, 158
The Book of Wilding, 265
boulders, 19, 108, 245, 294
Boulton, Julia, 9, 226, 230, 231, 234
Bouteloua gracilis 'Honeycomb', 38, 133
Brakelights® redflower false yucca, 176
'Bristol Fairy' baby's breath, 174
brown-belted bumblebee, 42, 131
Bruce, Jonny, 236, 240, 245, 247
Buck, Griffith, 196
buckeye butterfly, 130
BUGA, 145
bulbs, 192
bumblebee, 42, 281
Bunting, Andrew, 8, 62–75
bur oak, 294
Burrell, Charlie, 260, 264
butterflies, 16, 58, 70, 116, 133, 161, 204, 281
'Butterfly Magnet' meadow blazing star, 42, 122
butterfly milkweed, 24, 38, 46, 55, 76, 149, 156, 160

C
cabbage white butterfly, 128
cacti, 62, 172
Calamagrostis × acutiflora 'Karl Foerster', 296
calamint, 24, 25, 42, 55, 112, 120, 156, 196, 199, 210
Calamintha nepeta ssp. *nepeta*, 24, 25, 55
California poppy, 66, 80, 216, 245
Calylophus hybrid 'WNCYLASUN', Ladybird® Sunglow, 174
Campanula patula, 264
candelabrum sage, 253
cardinal flower, 196, 199
Carex brevior, 24, 303
Carthusian pink, 25, 114, 130, 133, 158
castor bean, 219
Catananche caerulea 'Tizi-n-Test', 256
caterpillars, 116
catmint, 62, 196, 199, 280
Ceanothus americanus, 116
cedar waxwing, 156
"Celebrating New American Gardens" exhibit, 200, 209
century agave, 174
cereus cactus, 184
Chanticleer Garden, 8, 62, 76, 180–195
Chatto, Andrew, 226, 234
Chatto, Beth, 7, 8, 62, 136, 140, 226–235, 236
Chattowood, 9, 234, 235
"Chelsea chop," 26
Chicago, IL, 8–9, 122–135, 302
Chicago Botanic Garden, 62, 102
chionodoxa, 156
chipmunk, 27
chokeberry, 62
cholla, 166
City of Madison Waterworks, 108–121
cliff goldenrod, 25
climates, 100
Collins, Keith, 236–247
'Color Guard' Adam's needle, 204
columbine, 216
common buckeye caterpillar, 161
common foxglove, 242
common milkweed, 112, 284
community, 128
competitors, 216
coneflower, 12, 46, 55, 76, 80, 82, 85, 126, 139, 152, 156, 214, 217, 286, 289, 294, 302
Conway, Sean, 8, 76–90
Conwell, Bill, 62
coreopsis, 12, 155, 156, 286
Coreopsis lanceolata, 24, 158
Coreopsis palmata, 26, 160, 284
Coreopsis verticillata 'Zagreb', 102
cornflower, 236
corporate campuses, 9
Corydalis lutea, 25, 26
Coryphantha vivipara, 174
Cotinus coggygria 'NCC01', Winecraft Black®, 54
cotoneaster, 170
Cotoneaster dammeri 'Streibs Findling', 178
Coulter's Matilija poppy, 230, 232
Country Landscapes, 34
COVID-19 pandemic, 62, 64, 66, 76, 252
Crassula perfoliata var. *falcata*, 191
Crawley, Mick, 264
'Cream' California poppy, 84
Creative Folkestone, 240
creeping buttercup, 62
creeping juniper, 178
Cretian pincushion flower, 256
CROCUS (Community Research on Climate and Urban Science), 302
cues for care, 25, 36, 50

Cultivating Life (TV show), 8, 76, 79
Cunningham, Linda, 46
Cunningham, Mike, 8, 46–61
cup plant, 112
cutting back plants, 23, 26, 99, 280
Cylindropuntia imbricata var. *arborescens*, 170

D
daffodil, 16, 155, 156, 158, 192, 214
Dalea purpurea, 116, 117, 128
The Damp Garden (Chatto), 230
'Dark Towers' beardtongue, 24, 58
Deam's black-eyed Susan, 96, 103, 117
deer, 66, 70, 102, 116, 296
deer-footed mouse, 27
Delos Garden, 9, 248–259
Delosperma 'John PJS02S', 193
Delosperma 'John Proffitt', 193, 195
demonstration gardens, 202
dense blazing star, 133
depth of gravel, 68
Derek Jarman's Garden (Jarman), 236, 241
design considerations, 18, 19, 82
dianthus, 126, 196, 199, 236
Dianthus carthusianorum, 25, 114, 130, 133
Diblik, Roy, 7, 8, 54, 122, 126, 136, 152, 162, 196, 290–305
donkey tail spurge, 70, 73
dragonfly, 260
driftwood, 236, 242
driveways, 145
drought, 16, 118, 184, 226
drumlins, 34, 39, 40
The Dry Garden (Chatto), 230
dry landscapes, 136, 147
Dungeness, England, 9, 236–247
'Durango Spineless' beavertail cactus, 174

E
eastern carpenter bee, 219
eastern prickly pear, 70
eastern red cedar, 92, 156
eastern white pine, 294
East Friesland meadow sage, 130
Echeveria × *gigantea*, 188, 191
Echeveria 'Afterglow', 191
echinacea, 139
Echinacea pallida, 54, 133, 218, 280, 284
Echinacea paradoxa, 160, 280
Echinacea purpurea, 280
Echinacea purpurea 'Baby Swan White', 303
Echinacea purpurea 'Green Jewel', 84
Echinacea purpurea 'PAS702917', PowWow® Wild Berry, 54
Echinacea purpurea 'Pica Bella', 116
Echinacea tennesseensis, 24, 54, 55, 160
Echinops ritro, 160
Echinops sphaerocephalus, 174
edging, 19, 36, 50, 60, 69, 133, 294
educational signage, 36, 202
Eischeid, Austin, 294
elephant hawk moth, 260
'Elijah Blue' fescue, 189
Elwood (gnome), 196
Emilia coccinea, 84
English longhorn cattle, 260
environmental benefits, 12
Epic Systems, 8, 9, 276–289, 290
Epping, Jeff, 46–61, 62, 66, 108, 112, 126, 152–165, 196, 276–289, 294
Eragrostis spectabilis, 102, 281
Erigeron annuus, 265
Eryngium planum 'Blaukappe', 188
Eryngium yuccifolium, 42, 80, 158, 160, 218, 296
Eschscholzia californica 'Cream', 84
Essex, England, 9, 62, 226–235
Eupatorium hyssopifolium, 296
euphorbia, 146
Euphorbia characias ssp. *wulfenii*, 188
Euphorbia corollata, 26, 160
Euphorbia myrsinites, 70, 178
Euphorbia 'Nothowlee', BLACKBIRD, 71
Euphorbia rigida, 256
Euphorbia tirucalli, 191
Eurybia × *herveyi* 'Twilight', 38
Eutrochium maculatum, 202, 206
evergreens, 36
Exmoor ponies, 200, 205

F
false indigo, 46, 55, 92, 216
FASLA (Solutions in the Land), 290
Faulkner, Judy, 276
feather grass, 210, 294
fencing, 36
fertilizers, 99
Festuca glauca 'Elijah Blue', 189
'Feuerland' yarrow, 25
field sparrow, 284
Filippi, Olivier, 252, 254
Fitzpatrick, Reshorna, 122–135
'Floristan White' blazing star, 34, 39, 180
flowering spurge, 26, 160
flying squirrel, 27
fountains, 8, 76, 108–121
foxes, 27
foxtail lily, 26
fritillaries, 26
Froggatt, Nigel, 252
Fuller, Zane, 280, 281, 284

G
'Garden Ghost' white sage, 130
Gates, Theaster, 122
gaura, 76, 196, 199
gayfeather, 302
'Georgia Pancake' fringed blue star, 174
geranium, 92, 94, 103
Geranium × *cantabrigiense* 'Karmina', 106
German statice, 16

giant coneflower, 158
giant mullein, 234
'Gibraltar' Thunberg bush clover, 287
'Ginger Love' fountain grass, 206
Glandularia canadensis, 218
Glas, Adam, 8, 92, 96, 101
globe thistle, 160, 166, 168
glory-of-the-snow, 12
glyphosate, 18
goat pruning, 253
golden oat grass, 85
Golden oats, 84, 178
golden poppy, 238
'Golden Prairie prairie dropseed, 39
goldenrod, 12, 46, 55, 126, 156, 158
Golden Sunset® yellow prairie grass, 34, 40
goldfinch, 160, 284
'Gold Nugget' hens and chicks, 172
Goodman Pool, 108–121
gorse, 236
grama grass, 46, 55
Granita Orange® ice plant, 193
granite, 68, 136
granite chip gravel, 19
grape hyancith, 192, 214
grasses, 12, 16, 34, 80, 112, 147, 212, 286
grasshoppers, 116
gravel, 68, 100. *See also specific types of gravel*
gravel calculators, 18
gravel culture, 101
gravel gardening
- aesthetics, 36
- basics, 18–23
- with bulbs, 192
- defined, 7
- frequently asked questions, 99–101
- green roofs, 282
- planter, 114
- raised bed, 114
- as renovation, 82, 100
- in troughs, 172
- updating established gardens, 158

gravel layer, 19, 21, 68
gray squirrel, 27
great black wasp, 58
great burnet, 66
Great Dixter, 240
great globe thistle, 175
Great Migration Greenway, 302
Grecian horehound, 256
Greencorps Chicago, 122, 126
greenhouses, 80, 221
'Green Jewel' purple coneflower, 84
green roofs, 282
Gregers-Warg, Åsa, 230, 231, 232
'Grey Owl' red cedar, 105
Grime, J. Philip, 216
gulf fritillary, 218
Gypsophila paniculata 'Bristol Fairy', 174

H

Hager, Jackie, 276, 280, 281, 284, 287
hairy penstemon, 16
'Happy Days' sunflower, 102
Harpur, Charlie, 260–275
Hawke, Richard, 102
hedgehog cactus, 172
Helianthus 'Happy Days', 102
hell strips, 46
hens and chicks, 66, 172
herbicides, 18
Hermannshof, 7, 8, 92, 101, 136–150, 290
'Herrenhausen' ornamental oregano, 116, 172, 174
Hershey, Ben, 34
Hesperaloe parviflora 'Perpa', Brakelights®, 176
Hetrick, Kara, 200
hibiscus, 196, 199
Hillside Water-wise Garden, 8, 196–209
Hitchmough, James, 264
hoary vervain, 161
Holm, Heather, 58
'Holy Smoke' big bluestem, 34, 40, 42
Homan Grown, 122, 126
Homegrown National Park, 36
homeowners associations (HOAs), 46, 52
honey bee, 160
'Honeycomb' blue grama grass, 34, 38, 39, 133
honeywort, 253
hornbeam, 80, 87
Hubricht's bluestar, 62, 96, 206
'Hummelo' betony, 102
hummingbirds, 116
hummingbird trumpet, 176
Hydrangea paniculata 'Limelight', 54
Hylotelephium 'Matrona', 204
hyssop-leaf thoroughwort, 296

I

ice plant, 66, 184
ikebana (Japanese flower arranging), 226, 230
insects, 27, 50, 116, 156, 266, 271, 300
Intrinsic Perennials, 126
invasive species, 62
Iowa State University, 8, 30, 188, 196–209
iris, 170
ironweed, 46, 55, 62, 66
irrigation, 22
'Isla Gold' tansy, 70
'Ivory Queen' ornamental onion, 193, 195

J

Jabco, Jeff, 8, 92, 101
Jarman, Derek, 9, 226, 230, 236–247
Jaugstetter, Bettina, 8, 140, 142
'J.C. Raulston' Parry's agave, 71
Jekyll, Gertrude, 248
Jenkintown, PA, 166–179
Jensen, Jens, 126
joe-pye weed, 196, 199, 202, 206, 214, 216, 294

junco, 284
juniper, 62, 182
Juniperus horizontalis 'Pancake', 178
Juniperus virginiana 'Glauca', 156
Juniperus virginiana 'Grey Owl', 105
Juniperus virginiana 'Taylor', 184

K
'Karl Foerster' feather read grass, 184
'Karmina' geranium, 106
Kent, England, 9, 248–259
Kentucky coffee tree, 92
Kenwood Gardens, 122
king's spear, 195
Kintzley, William, 188
'Kintzley's Ghost' grape honeysuckle, 184, 188–189
Knepp, Eric, 112
Knepp Castle, 9, 140, 260–275
Kniphofia, 26, 102
Korean feather grass, 184
'Kudos Mandarin' hummingbird mint, 204

L
Ladybird® Sunglow Texas primrose, 174
lambs' ear, 76, 85, 196, 199
lanceleaf coreopsis, 24, 158
landscape fabric, 99
Lavandula × *intermedia* 'Niko', PHENOMENAL, 70
Lavandula angustifolia 'Munstead', 204
lava rock, 140
lavender, 16, 62, 76, 80, 82, 85, 152
lavender cotton, 188, 240
lawn strips and patches, 36, 46, 50, 62
lead plant, 116, 156
Lemont, IL, 290–305
Leon, Annamaria, 122–135, 294, 302
Lespedeza thunbergii 'Gibraltar', 287
lesser celandine, 62
Leucanthemum vulgare, 265
Liatris aspera, 280
Liatris ligulistylis, 130
Liatris ligulistylis 'Butterfly Magnet', 122
Liatris pycnostachya, 284
Liatris spicata, 133
Liatris spicata 'Floristan Weiss', 180
Liatrus aspera, 105
'Limelight' panicle hydrangea, 54
limestone, 68, 70, 252, 253, 294
Limonium latifolium, 116
'Linda anise hyssop, 84
Linda Valentine Memorial Garden, 46–61
Lindera glauca var. *salicifolia*, 73
little bluestem, 12, 46, 55, 66, 76, 80, 92, 103, 112, 116, 120, 156, 196, 199, 280, 284, 286
'Little Spire' Russian sage, 54, 55, 297
Lloyd, Christopher, 226, 230, 236, 240
Lomelosia cretica, 256
longevity, 100
Lonicera reticulata 'Kintzley's Ghost', 188–189
low-impact gardening, 196
Lunaria annua 'Corfu Blue', 256
Lyon, Ed, 8, 196–209

M
Madagascar ocotillo, 191
Madison, WI, 8, 12–29, 46–61, 108–121, 152–165
maintenance, 22, 23, 99, 114
Mamie Till-Mobley Forgiveness Garden, 122, 302
Manor House ornamental oregano, 84
Marano, John, 166
marjoram, 172, 240, 245
'Matrona' stonecrop, 204
McCracken, Ana, 9, 30–45
McCracken, Ed, 30–45
McCrumb, Megan, 108
McVicar, Jekka, 264
meadow blazing star, 130
Meadowbrook Farm, 166–179
meadow sage, 85, 94, 103
Meanwhile Garden, 234, 235
medians, 98, 140, 145
medicinal plants, 240, 245
Mediterranean Garden Society, 248
Mediterranean spurge, 180, 184, 188
Mediterranean wild thyme, 256
Melica ciliata, 256
mental health, 128
Mexican feather grass, 76, 85, 149, 178, 193, 218
Mexican hat, 38
Mexican hens and chicks hybrid, 188
'Midnight Oil' eastern bee balm, 38
Midwest Groundcovers, 126
milkweed bugs, 39, 103
'Millennium' ornamental onion, 70, 96
Modern Nature (Jarman), 236, 240, 241
Molinia arundinacea 'Skyracer', 158
Molinia caerulea ssp. *arundinacea* 'Skyracer', 64
monarch butterfly, 38, 39, 42, 160, 296
monarda, 126
Monarda bradburiana 'Midnight Oil', 38
Monarda punctata, 40
moon carrot, 180, 184, 187, 188
moonshine yarrow, 130
Moore, Darryl, 234
moor grass, 62
mountain aloe, 191
mountain mint, 210
Mt. Cuba Center, 116, 284
mulch, 100, 140, 210
mullein, 76, 85
Muscari armeniacum, 192
Muscari armeniacum 'Valerie Finnis', 192
Myrtillocactus geometrizans, 191
myrtle spurge, 178

N
Nacogdoches, TX, 210–224
Narcissus 'Hawera', 192

Nassauer, Joan, 36, 50
Nassella tenuissima, 178, 193, 218
National Wildlife Federation, 36
needle-leaved blue star, 58
negative space, 66, 75, 76, 180
Nepeta racemosa, 280
New Jersey tea, 116
'New Moon' ornamental onion, 131, 133
New York Times, 66
Nicolson, Harold, 248, 252
nigella, 253
nightingale, 272
nodding onion, 42, 161
nodding yucca, 180
Norris, Kelly, 9, 30–45
North American Prairie Garden, 7, 139, 149
Northwind Perenial Farm, 126, 290
'Northwind' switch grass, 54, 204, 206

O

'October Skies' aromatic aster, 54, 296
Olbrich Botanical Gardens, 8, 46, 62, 108, 112, 115, 118, 152–165, 294
Oostvaardersplassen, 260
Opuntia basilaris 'Beavertail', 188
Opuntia basilaris 'Durango Spineless', 174
Opuntia humifusa, 70
Opuntia polyacantha, 70
'Orange Emperor' tulip, 192
Orchard Meadow, 253
Origanum laevigatum, 256
Origanum laevigatum 'Herrenhausen', 84, 116, 172, 174
Origanum libanoticum, 172
orlaya, 180, 184
ornamental grasses, 155, 156
ornamental onion, 12, 16, 46, 55, 94, 120, 152, 156, 192, 199, 302
ornamental oregano, 256
Oudolf, Piet, 7, 136
owls, 27
ox-eye daisy, 238, 265

P

painted turtle, 80
pale purple coneflower, 16, 218, 280, 284, 294
Panicum virgatum, 284
Panicum virgatum 'Northwind', 54, 204, 206
Panicum virgatum 'Ruby Ribbons', 296
Panicum virgatum 'Shenandoah', 54
parking garages, 276–289
parking lots, 96, 105, 108–121, 166, 226, 229
Parry's agave, 180
Parthenium integrifolium, 24, 70, 128, 130, 284
partridge feather, 174, 256
paths, 36, 40, 50, 73, 76, 87, 152, 199, 200, 283
patios, 73
pea gravel, 19, 34, 38, 68, 76, 87, 172, 188, 296
pearly everlasting, 70
Pearson, Dan, 248–259
Peckham, Samantha, 152, 156
Pennisetum alopecuroides 'Ginger Love', 206
Pennock, J. Liddon, Jr., 170
Pennsylvania Department of Transportation, 92
Pennsylvania Horticultural Society, 62, 66, 170
penstemon, 214, 236, 238, 286
Penstemon barbatus 'Coccineus', 264
Penstemon cobaea, 264
Penstemon 'Dark Towers', 24, 58
Penstemon digitalis, 296
Penstemon digitalis 'Pocahontas', 160
Penstemon grandiflorus, 264
Penstemon ovatus, 264
perennials, 12, 62, 73, 116, 126, 140, 147, 155, 166, 205, 264, 268
Perovskia atriplicifolia, 116, 178, 206, 296
Perovskia atriplicifolia 'Little Spire', 55, 297
Peruvian feather grass, 184
Phenomenal® lavender, 70
physical health, 128
'Pica Bella' purple coneflower, 116
pincushion cactus, 174
pine-leaved penstemon, 166, 168
pink hummingbird mint, 166, 168
place genius, 30
plains oval sedge, 303
plains prickly pear, 70
plan diagrams, 18, 19, 82
plant calculators, 18
planter gravel gardens, 114
Plantery, 210–224
plants
  cutting back, 23, 26, 99, 280
  depth, 99
  diversity, 140, 158, 165, 216
  establishing, 22
  heights, 50
  ideal size, 100
  native, 141, 214
  planting, 21, 114
  replanting, 158
  selecting, 21
  sourcing, 82
  spacing, 21, 92, 99, 101, 140
  survival strategies, 216
Plectocephalus americanus, 84
'Pocahontas' beardtongue, 160
pollinators, 12, 16, 40, 50, 58, 102, 131, 133, 140–141, 158, 160, 265, 287, 296
poppy, 76, 85, 236, 245, 253
poppy mallow, 195
Populus tremuloides, 39
porphyry gravel, 136
'Powis Castle' wormwood, 192
PowWow® Wild Berry coneflower, 54
prairie baby's breath, 16, 160
prairie blazing star, 184, 284
prairie clover, 156
prairie coreopsis, 112, 120

prairie dock, 16, 32, 39, 76, 85, 152, 158
prairie dropseed, 12, 16, 46, 55, 112, 120, 155, 156, 216, 217, 280, 286, 294, 302
prairie grasses, 126, 152
Prairie Rainwater Parkway Garden, 302
prairie sedge, 24
Prentis, Saffron, 252, 256
prickly cholla, 166
prickly pear cactus, 62, 166, 168, 170
privacy borders, 34
Pronschinske, Avery, 8, 152, 156, 165
propeller plant, 191
Prospect Cottage, 236–247
public spaces, 8
purple beech, 80, 87
purple coneflower, 120, 280
purple emperor butterfly, 272
purple love grass, 92, 102, 281
purple prairie clover, 16, 92, 103, 112, 116, 117, 120, 128
'Purple Sensation' ornamental onion, 102, 106
Pycnanthemum flexuosum, 102
Pycnanthemum tenuifolium, 70

Q

quaking aspen, 34, 39
quartzite gravel, 19, 50, 54, 60, 116, 130, 200, 204, 284
'Queen Fabiola' triplet lily, 192, 193
'Queen Nectarine' hummingbird mint, 176

R

rabbits, 16, 27, 54, 58, 116, 160, 281, 296
ragstone, 252, 256
rain gardens, 100, 152, 162, 196
raised bed gravel gardens, 114
Ratibida columnifera, 38
rattlesnake master, 34, 40, 42, 76, 80, 85, 152, 158, 160, 218, 296
'Raydon's Favorite' aromatic aster, 184
Rebuild Foundation, 122
'Red Cauli' sedum, 230, 232
red hot poker, 102
red oak, 294
'Red October' big bluestem, 296
red pencil tree, 191
Reiman Gardens, 8, 196–209
renovation, 82, 100
replanting, 158
reseeding, 140
reticulated iris, 192
reverse volcano, 83
Rewilded Garden, 260–275
Ricinus communis, 219
river rock, 68
Robinson, William, 248
rockrose, 240
Rodefeld, Dan, 108
roof gardens, 276–289
Roper, Lisa, 8, 180–195
rosemary, 240, 245
roses, 236
rose verbena, 218
rough goldenrod, 216
roundabouts, 8, 92–107, 140
royal catchfly, 84, 176
Royal Horticultural Society, 230
'Ruby Ribbons' switch grass', 296
Rudbeckia × 'American Gold Rush', 297
Rudbeckia × 'Sweet as Honey', 38
Rudbeckia fulgida 'Blovi', VIETTE'S LITTLE SUZY, 55
Rudbeckia fulgida var. *deamii*, 103, 117
Rudbeckia maxima, 158
ruderals, 216
'Rudy' triplet lily, 193
Ruellia humilis, 102
Ruin Garden, 180, 191
Rummery, Sarah, 200
Russian sage, 46, 55, 112, 116, 120, 152, 178, 206, 234, 294, 296
rusty patched bumble bee, 158

S

Sackville-West, Vita, 248, 252, 253
sage, 240, 245
salvia, 76, 80, 82, 92, 136, 146, 196, 199, 210, 219
Salvia argentea, 192, 195
Salvia interrupta, 253
Salvia nemorosa 'Ostfriesland', 130
sandstone, 73
Sanguisorba officinalis 'Tanna', 84
santolina, 236
Santolina chamaecyparissus, 188
'Sapphire Skies' beaked yucca, 174, 191
scabiosa, 180
Scabiosa cretica, 256
Schizachyrium scoparium, 80, 116, 280, 284
Schizachyrium scoparium 'MinnBlueA', BLUE HEAVEN, 102
Schmidt, Cassian, 7, 8, 92, 101, 103, 136–150, 290
Scott Arboretum, 62, 92
sculptures, 36, 82
sea holly, 66, 184
sea kale, 180, 236, 242
sea lavender, 116
seating, 36, 73, 152, 202, 300
sedum, 147, 172, 196, 199
Sedum × 'Sunset Boulevard', 130
Sedum rupestre 'Plum Dazzled', 193, 195
Sedum sediforme, 256
self-sowing/self-seeding, 158, 160, 180, 184, 214
Sempervivum, 172
Senna hebecarpa, 54
Seseli gummiferum, 187, 188
Sesleria autumnalis, 24, 296
shade, 99, 100
sharp-shinned hawk, 27
'Shenandoah' switch grass, 54
showy milkweed, 16
sidewalks, 96, 98
Sievert, Linda, 276, 283

signage, educational, 36, 82, 202
Silene regia, 84, 176
silky-spike melic grass, 256
Silphium terebinthinaceum, 85, 158
silver feather grass, 230, 232
silver sage, 180, 184, 192, 195
Sissinghurst Castle, 9, 248–259
site selection, 18
size of gravel, 68
skipper butterfly, 54, 116
skyblue aster, 281
'Skyracer' moor grass, 62, 64, 76, 85
slender mountain mint, 70
Smitt, Troy Scott, 248–259
smokebush, 256
smooth aster, 284
snapping turtle, 80
sneezeweed, 196, 199
snow removal, 114
soaptree yucca, 187
soil enhancement, 128
soil removal, 100
'Solar Fire' ursinia, 193
soldier beetle, 130
Solidago × 'Sugar Kisses', 130
Solidago drummondii, 25
Solidago 'Wichita Mountains', 287
songbirds, 27, 284
song sparrow, 156
southern magnolia, 170
spacing, 21, 92, 99, 101, 140
Spinelli Barracks, 140, 145
Spirits in the Garden, 200, 209
Sporobolus heterolepis, 280
spotted bee balm, 40
Springer, Lauren, 191
spurge, 62, 66, 76, 85, 156, 170, 196, 199
squill, 158
Stachys byzantina 'Big Ears', 204
Stachys officinalis 'Hummelo', 102
staking, 19, 21, 210
'Standing Ovation' little bluestem, 34, 39
star-of-Bethlehem, 62
Stefko, Bob, 8
Stephen F. Austin State University (SFASU), 8, 210–224
Stipa gigantea, 84, 178
stonecrop, 256
'Streibs Finding' bearberry cotoneaster, 178
stress tolerators, 216
Stuart-Smith, Tom, 264
succulents, 62, 172, 180
sulphur butterfly, 42, 54
'Summer Beauty' ornamental onion, 24, 117, 160
'Summer Breeze' gaura, 184
'Summer's Swan Song' ironweed, 296
'Sunset Boulevard' sedum, 130
Sunsparkler® 'Plum Dazzled' stonecrop, 193, 195
survival strategies for plants, 216
swamp oak, 294
Swarthmore, PA, 62–75, 92–107
Swarthmore College, 8, 62, 92–107
'Sweet as Honey' black-eyed Susan, 38
switch grass, 46, 55, 92, 103, 210, 214, 284
Symphyotrichum laeve, 284
Symphyotrichum oblongifolium 'October Skies', 54, 296
Symphyotrichum oolentangiense, 281

T
Table Mountain® ice plant, 193, 195
Tallamy, Doug, 36
tall moor grass, 158
Tamworth pigs, 260
Tanacetum densum ssp. *amani*, 174, 256
Tanacetum vulgare 'Isla Gold', 70
'Tanna' greater burnet, 84
tassel flower, 76, 84
Tate, 240
'Taylor' eastern red cedar, 34, 36, 37, 184
teasel, 236, 242
temperatures, 100, 214
Tennessee coneflower, 24, 55, 112, 160, 184
terraces, 196–209, 248–259
Texas bluebonnet, 216
Texas primrose, 166, 168
Theory and Computing Sciences Building (TCS), 290–305
Thomas, Bill, 184
threadleaf coreopsis, 92, 103, 302
Thymbra capitata, 256
thyme, 76, 85
tickseed, 16, 26, 160, 284
tidiness, 36
Till, Emmett, 302
Till-Mobley, Mamie, 302
Timberland, 302
Tiverton, RI, 76–90
toadflax, 80
Tower Garden, 152, 156
Tree, Isabella, 260, 264
tree cholla, 170
triplet lily, 192
Triteleia 'Queen Fabiola', 192, 193
Triteleia 'Rudy', 193
troughs, 170, 172, 191
Trust for Public Land, 302
tulip, 16, 156, 158, 192
Tulipa 'Orange Emperor', 192
tumble gravel, 92
turfgrass, 69
Turner Construction, 294
turtledove, 272
turtlehead, 196, 199
'Twilight' aster, 38
'Twilight Zone' little bluestem, 34, 39
twistleaf yucca, 70
types of gravel, 68, 100

U
University of Wisconsin-Madison, 196
upright myrtle spurge, 256
upright prairie coneflower, 34
urban green spaces, 128, 140, 141, 142, 276–289, 302. See also Adopt A Lot program
Ursinia anthemoides 'Solar Fire', 193
U.S. Botanic Gardens, 200, 209

V
vacant lots, 8–9, 122–135
valerian, 236, 238, 242
'Valerie Finnis' grape hyacinth, 192
VanHorn, Doug, 108, 110, 112, 115
variegated foxtail agave, 188
Vera, Frans, 260
verbena, 214
Verbena stricta, 161
Vernonia × 'Summer's Swan Song', 296
Verona, Wisconsin, 276–289
vervain, 234
viper's bugloss, 236, 242
VIRIDIS Design Group, 290
voles, 16, 281
Voran, Laurel, 180

W
walls, 36, 170, 178, 252
Ward, David, 226
washed gravel, 12
wasps, 58, 128
water conservation, 12
watering, 22, 96, 100, 108, 114, 214
water quality, 128
Wayne, Pennsylvania, 180–195
weed management, 12, 16, 18, 22, 69, 210
weeds, 62, 66, 68, 114, 280
weeping hemlock, 170
Weinheim, Germany, 92, 101, 136–150
western bumblebee, 287
West Sussex, England, 9, 260–275
white goldenrod, 130
white oak, 294
whorled milkweed, 38
'Wichita Mountains' goldenrod, 287
wild carrot, 234
Wilding (Tree), 260, 265
wildlife, 27, 42, 58, 271, 272, 289
wild petunia, 102, 103
wild quinine, 24, 66, 70, 128, 130, 284
wild senna, 54
Wilkie, Anna, 112, 118
wilting foliage, 22
Winecraft Black® smokebush, 54
Woodard, Teresa, 8
Woods, Chris, 180
wormwood, 234

Y
yarrow, 126, 147, 155, 156, 196, 199, 234, 256, 294
yellow coneflower, 149, 160, 280
yellow corydalis, 25, 26
Yocca, David, 122, 290–305
yucca, 62, 166, 168, 180, 284
Yucca elata, 187
Yucca filamentosa, 158, 284
Yucca filamentosa 'Color Guard', 46, 50, 204
Yucca rostrata 'Sapphire Skies', 174, 191
Yucca rupicola, 70

Z
'Zagreb' threadleaf coreopsis, 102
Zauschneria garrettii, 176
zinnia, 219

BOB STEAK

JEFF EPPING's passion for plants and gardening is reflected in his thirty-five-year career as an award-winning horticulturist and garden designer. During his twenty-eight years as director of horticulture at Olbrich Botanical Gardens, he transformed a lawn-laden landscape into a nationally acclaimed public garden, known for its artistic and innovative, plant-driven designs and ecologically sound gardening techniques. Alongside that role, he also ran his own design and consulting business for twenty-five years and continues to do so today, specializing in eco-conscious designs for projects ranging from small home gardens to expansive business campuses. Jeff generously shared his expertise through hundreds of classes, workshops, tours, and lectures. His insightful writing has been featured in leading gardening publications like *Fine Gardening* and *Better Homes & Gardens*, and his work has been recognized by the *New York Times* and *Washington Post*, among others. Beyond print, he's also contributed to radio, television, online videos, and podcasts. He has received prestigious awards from both the American Public Gardens Association and the Perennial Plant Association, honoring his significant contributions to horticulture. Beyond gardening, Jeff enjoys spending time with his family, outdoor sports, hiking, hunting, foraging, and woodworking in his shop, where he continues to cultivate his love for nature and craftsmanship.

BRIAN WOODARD

TERESA WOODARD, an award-winning garden writer, brings a background in magazine writing and gardening experience. She is author of *Garden to the Max: Joyful, Visionary, Maximalist Design* (Timber Press, 2025) and co-author of *American Roots: Lessons and Inspiration from the Designers Reimagining Our Home Gardens* (Timber Press, 2022). During her sixteen-year writing career, she has written and produced garden content for regional and national publications including *Better Homes & Gardens* and *Country Gardens* and currently serves as contributing garden editor at *Midwest Living* magazine and content creator for digital garden media. She has won Gold and Silver Media Awards from GardenComm. Outside of work, she gardens at her home near Columbus, Ohio; volunteers at an urban garden teaching youth about growing food; and advises America in Bloom communities across the country.

BOB STEFKO is a Chicago-based photographer with a career that spans almost twenty-five years in both editorial and commercial work. During that time, he has photographed a diverse range of subjects, including many of this country's finest gardens, *Fortune* 500 CEOs, Olympic athletes, and some of the world's most remote landscapes. His work has appeared in hundreds of publications including *Better Homes & Gardens*, *Forbes*, *Wine Spectator*, and *Midwest Living* magazine, to name a few. Bob has completed two books on travel and food for Globe Pequot and Meredith Corporation and has received both Gold and Silver Media Awards from GardenComm. His most recent book, *Garden to the Max: Joyful, Visionary, Maximalist Design* (Timber Press, 2025), is a collaboration with Teresa Woodard. When not snapping pictures, you can usually find him living his secret life as a general contractor, being an urban gardener and wannabe chef, tinkering in his basement shop, hunting down mid-century modern treasures, or cycling the early mornings away on Lake Michigan. Bob and his wife, Shelby, live in their personally renovated 1890s house in the Rogers Park neighborhood of Chicago.